THE RIGHTS
OF THE READER

—

DANIEL PENNAC

illustrations and foreword by
QUENTIN BLAKE

translated by Sarah Adams

CANDLEWICK PRESS
CAMBRIDGE, MASSACHUSETTS

Text copyright © 1992 by Daniel Pennac
Translation copyright © 2006 by Sarah Adams
Illustrations and foreword copyright © 2006 by Quentin Blake

First U.S. edition 2008

Originally published in France as *Comme un roman* by Gallimard Jeunesse

Library of Congress Cataloging-in-Publication Data

Pennac, Daniel.
The rights of the reader / Daniel Pennac. —1st U.S. ed.
p.   cm.
ISBN 978-0-7636-3801-6
[1. Books and reading—France. 2. Fiction—Psychological aspects.]
I. Title.
Z1003.P3913 2008
028'.90944—dc22   2007052882

2 4 6 8 10 9 7 5 3 1

Printed in the United States of America

This book was typeset in Manticore.
The illustrations were done in pen and ink.

Candlewick Press
2067 Massachusetts Avenue
Cambridge, Massachusetts 02140

visit us at www.candlewick.com

For Franklin Rist,
a great reader of novels
and a reader worthy of a novel

—

To the memory of my father,
and in daily remembrance
of Frank Vlieghe

FOREWORD

There may seem to be something a bit crazy about writing an introduction to a book that has been in print for sixteen years and sold over a million copies in several languages. Even so, I hope there may be one or two footnotes that this Englishman and escaped school-teacher can usefully add to *The Rights of the Reader*.

Daniel Pennac is one of the best known and most successful writers in France today. His extraordinary imagination, occasionally bizarre humor, and gifts as a storyteller have ensured that all his novels are best sellers; so are his stories for children, and when, in 1992, as a former teacher, he came to write this book about young people and reading, it proved to be no exception.

What you have in your hands is a new translation by Sarah Adams and, it seems to me, a remarkably confident and sustaining one. She does Pennac with, if I can be allowed a couple of extra French words, élan and panache. What she doesn't do, with the profoundest of intentions, is attempt to translate the furniture and fittings of the culture from which the book arises. When Pennac refers to *Madame Bovary*, she doesn't attempt to substitute *David Copperfield* or *Vanity Fair*, and the text is a weave of local references, from newspapers such as *France Soir* and *L'Équipe*, children's books such as *Babar* and

Marcel Aymé's *Les contes du chat perché*, paperback series such as Le Livre de Poche and La Bibliothèque Verte, through to the fact that French children call their parents Maman and Papa. And what Daniel Pennac says about education relates to the organization of the French system and how French examinations work.

Of course, we hope that the reader to whom all this is unfamiliar will find it informative and flavorsome, but the last element, education, is of special importance because Pennac's reaction to it spurs him to argument and demonstration. The French approach to education has been essentially centralized, logical. There is a steely respect for the intellect (so, for instance, a teacher in a French secondary school is there exclusively to teach his or her subject, not to be responsible for discipline), and in order that pupils may get a taste of all of French literature, it is taught chronologically and using extracts or isolated poems. The possible failure of young readers to warm to reading within this constraining grid is one of the issues that Pennac addresses. The rights he demands are claims for liberty: you are allowed to skip bits, to read anything you like, maybe even, sometimes, not to read at all.

Perhaps the fact that I trained to be a teacher of English such a long time ago, in the fifties, broadly disqualifies me from taking part in the argument, but it does enable me to make one small observation. Presented with Pennac's book at that time, I'm not sure that my friends and I would have known what to do with it—I mean, most of us thought something like that already, didn't we?

It's rather chastening to discover that we have more need of it now. We know—people professionally involved in education know better than I do—that a creative approach can sometimes mean a neglect of standards, generally among those to whom standards were irksome anyway. By contrast, we are now in an era of tests and targets. There is nothing wrong with accountability; properly understood, we need it. What is disturbing is the withering effect of its demands when they are not properly understood. The French version of this is a rather dry respect for art and letters. In the U.K., and, as I understand it, in the U.S. as well, one senses not so much a respect for the subject as an urge to convert an elusive entity into something that can be tested. Am I just imagining it, or is there, behind all the tests and targets, a sort of fear of the rich, fluid diversity of the material—a fear, perhaps, among those who want to be in control at many levels of art and educational administration, that they cannot actually see or feel the substance they have put themselves in charge of? How satisfying, by contrast, the reassurance of a well-checked box.

In reaction to this, many well-known authors who write for children and young people have spoken up for a tradition of real books and real poems, one might almost say for real life. It is not surprising that teachers and librarians in Britain and the United States who are aware of Pennac's book should be eager to have this eloquent support from across the Channel and across the Atlantic readily available to them.

And now here it is. I don't want to get between you and it for any longer than it takes to observe how tonic and fortifying Daniel Pennac is, how positive; how, while researchers prepare their statistics, he reports on real life, dramatizes and relives it for us, so that we have a vivid sense of being addressed by a real writer, a real teacher, a real reader-aloud.

And of the possibilities he offers us.

QUENTIN BLAKE

Parents, teachers, librarians,
please on no account use these pages
as an instrument of torture.
D. P.

1
BIRTH OF THE ALCHEMIST

One

You can't make someone read. Just as you can't make them fall in love or dream. . . .

You can try, of course. "Go on, love me!" "Dream!" "Read! Read! Read, goddammit, I'm telling you to read!" "Go to your room and read!"

What happens next?

Nothing.

The young reader nods off over her book. The window suddenly looked, wide open, onto somewhere more tantalizing; she flew out that way to escape. But she sleeps warily: the book is still open in front of her. If we opened the bedroom door, we'd find her sitting at her desk, dutifully reading. Even if we tiptoed upstairs, she'd hear us coming.

"Do you like it, then?"

She can't say no. That would be a crime. Books are sacred; how can you not like reading? "No," she'll tell us, "the descriptions are too long."

Reassured, we head back down to the television. Her remark might even provoke a heated debate with our friends.

"She thinks the descriptions are too long. She's got a point, of course. We live in an audiovisual age, but the novelists of the nineteenth century had to describe everything. . . ."

"That's no reason to let them skip half the book!"

Why waste our energy? She's gone back to sleep.

— Two —

Young people's reluctance to read is all the harder to understand if you're of a generation, a time, a background, a family, where everyone always tried to keep you from reading.

"Stop reading, for goodness' sake—you'll strain your eyes!"

"Why don't you go outside and play? It's a beautiful day."

"Lights out! It's late!"

Yes, the weather was always too good for reading. And the night too dark.

It's interesting that even back then, reading was rarely a matter of choice. So it became a subversive act.

You didn't just discover a novel; you were disobeying your parents too. A double victory. The happy memory of reading time snatched under the bedclothes by flashlight. How fast Anna Karenina galloped toward her Vronsky in the dead of night! They were in love — how romantic. And they were in love in spite of the ban on reading — even better. They were in love in spite of Mom and Dad, math homework, a French essay, a bedroom that needed tidying. They were too in love to go down for supper. They loved each other more than dessert. They were too head over heels to join in the soccer game or go mushroom picking. They had chosen each other and preferred each other to anyone else. My God, how beautiful love is.

And how short that novel was.

— Three —

To be fair, we parents didn't set out to turn reading into a chore. All we thought about, in the beginning, was our children's enjoyment. We were in a state of grace during those early years. Our total sense of wonder in the face of a new life transformed us into geniuses. For them, we became storytellers. As soon as they emerged, blinking, into the world of language, we told them stories. It was a talent we didn't know we had. Their enjoyment inspired us. Their happiness gave us voice. We created character after character, adventure after adventure, ratcheting up the plots. We invented a whole world for them, much as the aging Tolkien did for his grandchildren. On the border of day and night, we became their novelist.

Not that it would have mattered if we'd had no talent for storytelling. If we'd told them other people's stories — badly, groping for words, mispronouncing names, mixing up adventures, muddling the beginning of one with the ending of another. . . . Even if we hadn't made up stories at all, if we'd just read aloud, we'd still have been their personal novelists, their special storytellers helping them slip into their dreamy pajamas every evening before dissolving under the sheets of night. More than that, we were the book.

Remember that intimacy. There's nothing like it.

How we loved scaring just for the thrill of consoling! And how desperately they wanted to be scared! They weren't fooled, even then, but they trembled all the same. They were real readers, in other words. What a playful partnership we formed: they the cunning readers, we the book!

— *Four* —

We taught our young readers everything about books before they knew how to read. We opened their minds to the infinite richness of imaginary things, introduced them to the joys of vertical travel; we gave them the power to go anywhere, delivered them from Chronos, plunged them into the fabulously crowded solitude of the reader. . . . The stories we read them were full of brothers, sisters, parents, imaginary twins, teams of guardian angels, fleets of special friends to protect them from their sorrows, but who in turn found protection from their own fictional demons in the worried beating of the children's hearts. The children became their reciprocal angels: readers. Without them, the characters' world could not exist. Without the characters, the children were weighed down by their own reality. And so they discovered the paradoxical virtue of reading, which is to abstract ourselves from the world in order to make sense of it.

They returned from these voyages unable to speak. It was morning, and we were moving on to something else. To be honest, we didn't really bother trying to find out what they'd brought back from the other side. Innocently, they cultivated this mystery. It was their own private world. Their personal relationship with Snow White, or

whichever of the Seven Dwarfs they were on close terms with, demanded secrecy. The reader's greatest pleasure: the silence after the story has been read.

Yes, we taught them everything about books.

As readers they were ready for anything.

So ready, and let's not forget this, they were desperate to learn how to read.

— Five —

What great teachers we were, when we didn't worry about our methods.

~ Six ~

Look at him now, years later, in his bedroom, with a book he's not reading. The urge to be somewhere else is a murky screen between him and the open page, blurring the lines. There he is, by the window, behind the closed door. Page forty-eight. He doesn't want to think about how long it's taken him to reach this forty-eighth page. The book contains exactly four hundred and forty-six of them. Call it five hundred. Five hundred pages! If only there were more dialogue. Not that it would make much difference. The pages are crammed with lines, squeezed between tiny margins, black paragraphs stacked on top of one another; here and there is the relief of a conversation—quotation marks, like an oasis, denoting one character talking to another. But the other person doesn't reply. And then there's a run of twelve pages. Twelve pages of black ink! It's suffocating. Totally suffocating. Fucking hell, he swears. Sorry, but he swears. Stupid-bloody-fucking-pile-of-shit-of-a-book. Page forty-eight . . . If only he could remember what those first forty-seven pages were about. But he doesn't dare ask himself the question that someone else is bound to put to him sooner or later.

The winter's night settles in. The theme music for the TV news rises through the floorboards. Another half hour till supper. Books are extraordinarily compact. You can't make a hole in them. And they're meant to be hard to burn. Fire can't get between the pages. Lack of oxygen. This is what our reader thinks about in the margins: his own exceedingly wide margins. A book is thick, compact, dense, a blunt instrument. Page forty-eight or one hundred forty-eight, what's the difference? The landscape's the same. He can see the teacher's lips mouthing the title. He can hear all his friends asking, "How many pages?"

"Three or four hundred."

(Liar.)

"When's it for?"

Naming the fateful day sets off a chorus of protest. "Two weeks? We've got to read four hundred" — five hundred — "pages in two weeks! But we'll never make it!"

The teacher is not about to negotiate.

A book is a blunt instrument and a block of eternity. It's the physical manifestation of boredom. A book. "The book." Students never call it anything else in their essays: the book, a book, the books, some books.

"In his book *Pensées,* Pascal tells us that . . ."

The teacher can use all the red ink he likes pointing out that it's not the right terminology. That you should talk about a novel, an essay, a collection of short stories, a volume of poetry. That the word *book* by itself means everything and nothing. A telephone directory is a book;

so is a dictionary, a travel guide, a stamp album, an accounts ledger. . . .

Nothing doing. The word will write itself again in their next essay.

"In his book *Madame Bovary,* Flaubert tells us that . . ."

Because, from their lonely perspective, a book is a book. And each book weighs down on them like an encyclopedia, the hardback kind we used to tuck under children's bottoms so they were high enough to reach the table.

Each time, the weight of the book gets the young reader down. They were lighthearted enough when they sat down just now— full of resolve. But after a few pages they were overwhelmed by the painfully familiar weight, by boredom, by unbearable effort, by all the going nowhere.

Their drooping eyelids warn of shipwreck any minute now.

Their resolve has foundered on the rock of page forty-eight.

The book drags them down. Together they sink.

— Seven —

Downstairs, around the TV, the argument about the corrupting power of television is gaining momentum.

"I just can't believe how stupid and vulgar and violent programs are today. You can't turn the television on without seeing . . ."

"Take Japanese animation. Have you ever *seen* a Japanese animation?"

"It's not just the programs; it's the medium itself. It's passive. It makes the viewer lazy."

"Yes, you switch it on, sit down . . ."

"You channel-hop."

"You can't focus on anything."

"At least that way you miss the ads."

"Doesn't work anymore. They've synchronized the programs. You escape one ad and end up watching another."

"Sometimes the same one!"

Silence: a shared moment of adult brilliance.

Then somebody, *mezza voce*: "But reading is different; reading is something you *do*."

"Absolutely, reading is active. 'The act of reading.' I couldn't agree more."

"But with TV, and movies for that matter, everything's handed to you on a plate; nothing has to be worked at;

they just spoon-feed you. The picture, the sound, the scenery, the atmospheric music in case you haven't understood what the director's up to . . ."

"The creaking door that tells you to be scared stiff . . ."

"You have to imagine it all when you're reading. . . . Reading is endlessly creative."

Silence again. (Between these endlessly creative people.)

Then: "What I find shocking is the average number of hours a kid spends watching TV compared to the number they spend in French lessons. I've seen the statistics."

"They must be staggering."

"One hour of French for every six or seven in front of the TV. And that's not counting going to the movies. A child (not ours, of course) spends on average two hours a day in front of the TV, eight to ten on weekends. Making a grand total of thirty-six hours, compared to five hours of French lessons per week."

"No wonder school can't compete."

A third silence.

This time at the thought of such an impossible gulf.

– Eight –

There are lots of things that can be said about the growing divide between the young reader and books.

We've said them all.

That television, for example, isn't the only problem.

That the decades separating our children's generation and our own youthful reading might as well be centuries.

So while we may feel we're psychologically closer to our children than our parents were to us, intellectually speaking we're closer to our parents.

(Here, there is heated debate about the terms *psychological* and *intellectual*. A new adverb is drafted in.)

"*Affectively* closer, if you like."

"Effectively?"

"I didn't say *e*ffectively; I said *a*ffectively."

"In other words, we're affectively closer to our children, but effectively closer to our parents, is that right?"

"Put it this way: our children are the sons and daughters of their time, while we were just our parents' children."

". . . ?"

"No, seriously. When we were growing up, we weren't consumers. Commercially and culturally speaking, we lived in a society of adults. Same clothes, same food, same culture. Little brother wore big brother's cast-offs. We ate the same food, at the same time and the same table, went on the same Sunday walks. Television brought the family together via one single channel (which was much better, by the way, than all the rubbish on today). And when it came to reading, the only thing our parents worried about was making sure certain books were out of reach."

"As for the previous generation, our grandparents' generation, girls were quite simply forbidden to read."

"Too right! Especially novels: 'imagination, the madwoman in the attic.' Bad for marriage, that kind of thing . . ."

"But teenagers today form an entirely separate category of consumers in a society that clothes, entertains, feeds, and cultivates them, where fast-food outlets and designer labels are booming. We went to parties; they go clubbing. We read books; they have headphones. The Beatles brought us closer together; they shut themselves off in the autistic world of their MP3 player. Nowadays, you even see the previously unimaginable: whole *quartiers* taken over by young people, giant tracts of urban landscape dedicated to 'hanging out.'"

It's at this point they mention the Pompidou Center.

Also known as the Beaubourg.

The barbarous Beaubourg . . .

Beaubourg, that teeming nightmare, Beaubourg-drugs-and-violence-and-hanging-out and that black hole of an RER station . . . watch out for the Hole at Les Halles!

"Spewing out illiterate hordes at the foot of the greatest public library in France!"

Silence again . . . a beautiful silence: the Angel of Paradox passes overhead.

"Do your children spend much time at the Beaubourg?"

"Hardly any. We're lucky enough to live in the fifteenth arrondissement."

Silence.

"Basically, they don't read anymore."

"No."

"Too many distractions."

"Yes."

— *Nine* —

And if it's not television, it's the consumer society gone mad or the electronic invasion. And if those hypnotic video games aren't to blame, then school is. The insane way they teach reading these days, the outmoded curriculum, incompetent teachers, dilapidated buildings, a shortage of libraries.

What else?

Oh, yes. The miserable budget for the cultural sector. And the infinitesimal sliver of that microscopic grant that is allocated to books.

How can you expect my daughter/my son/our children/young people to read in such conditions?

"Everyone is reading less, in any case."

"True."

~ Ten ~

And so we go on, language triumphing over the opacity of things, luminous silences that speak louder than words. We are watchful and knowledgeable; we are not taken in by the times we live in. The whole world informs what we say—and is illuminated by what we don't say. We are clear-sighted. We're fanatical about being clear-sighted.

So why does the conversation leave a faintly bitter aftertaste? Is it the silence of the house, empty again, only the dishes to do? A little way off, at the traffic lights, our friends are in the grip of the same silence. Their rush of lucidity over, they fall quiet in their stationary cars, as couples do on their way home from an evening out. Like a hangover, or like coming to from an anesthetic, slowly surfacing toward consciousness, clambering back into their own skins, the slightly painful sensation of not recognizing themselves in what they've said. We weren't there. Everything happened, of course, the arguments were valid—and, from that point of view, we were right—but *we weren't there*. No question about it, yet another evening spent, mind-numbingly, being right.

That's how it is—you think you're going home, but in fact you're being returned to your body.

What we were saying back then, at the dinner table, couldn't have been further removed from what our inner voices were telling us. We were talking about the importance of reading, but we were really with our young reader, upstairs in their bedroom, not reading. We were listing all the reasons why children don't like reading, but at the same time we were trying to cross the book gulf that separates them from us. We were talking about books, but we were thinking about our child.

He didn't help by coming down to supper at the last possible moment, parking his teenage moodiness at the table without a word of apology, and making no effort to join in the conversation. And after all that, he left before dessert.

"Got to go and read—sorry!"

– Eleven –

Lost intimacy . . . Thinking about it later, as our insomnia kicks in, we see that that ritual of reading every evening at the end of the bed when they were little—set time, set gestures—was like a prayer. A sudden truce after the battle of the day, a reunion lifted out of the ordinary. We savored the brief moment of silence before the storytelling began, then our voice, sounding like itself again, the liturgy of chapters. . . . Yes, reading a story every evening fulfilled the most beautiful, least selfish, and least speculative function of prayer: that of having our sins forgiven. We didn't confess, we weren't looking for a piece of eternity, but it was a moment of communion between us, of textual absolution, a return to the only paradise that matters: intimacy. Without realizing it, we were discovering one of the crucial functions of storytelling and, more broadly speaking, of art in general, which is to offer a respite from human struggle.

Love wore a new skin.

And it was free.

— *Twelve* —

Free. That was how our children experienced it. A gift. Time out. In spite of everything. The bedtime story relieved them of their daytime burdens. Freed from their moorings, they traveled with the wind, infinitely lighter. And the wind was our voice.

We asked nothing for the trip, nothing in return. It wasn't even a reward. (You always had to prove yourself worthy of a reward.) In this land, everything happened for free.

Gratis being the only currency in art.

– Thirteen –

So what happened between that intimacy and our teenagers now, hard up against a book cliff, as we try to understand them (meaning, put our own minds at rest) by blaming our century and television — which, by the way, we may have forgotten to switch off. . . .

Is it television's fault?

Was the twentieth century too visual? The nineteenth too descriptive? Why not the eighteenth too rational, the seventeenth too classical? Too much Renaissance in the 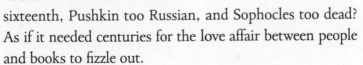 sixteenth, Pushkin too Russian, and Sophocles too dead? As if it needed centuries for the love affair between people and books to fizzle out.

A few years are enough.

A few weeks.

A misunderstanding.

When we used to sit at the end of their bed, conjuring up Little Red Riding Hood's dress and the contents of her basket down to the last detail — not forgetting the thickest part of the wood, or how strangely furry Grandmother's ears looked, or that small peg and the wooden latch—I don't remember them finding our descriptions too long.

It's not as if centuries have gone by since. Just those moments we call "life" but that seem like an eternity because we've taken it for granted that everyone must read.

– *Fourteen* –

In this, as in so many other ways, life turned out to be a falling away of pleasure. A year of telling stories at the end of their bed. Two years, perhaps. Three at a pinch. Based on a story an evening, that's a grand total of one thousand ninety-five stories. Not bad! And even if the story only took fifteen minutes, we'd always spend the same time again deciding which one to tell.

The trials and tribulations of inspiration . . .

At first, they helped. What their sense of wonderment required of us wasn't a story, but the *same* story.

"Again? You want *Tom Thumb* again? But *Tom Thumb* isn't the only story, sweetheart. Good heavens, there's . . ."

Tom Thumb—nothing else would do.

Who'd have thought that one day we'd long for that happy time when the sole inhabitant of their forest was Tom Thumb? For the time would come when we would curse ourselves for teaching them about variety, for giving them the choice.

"No, you've already told me that one!"

Although it doesn't quite take over our lives, choice becomes a headache. And our resolutions are short-lived: next Saturday, we say, we'll rush off to a specialist bookshop and scour the children's section. But Saturday gets put off until the following Saturday. Their fervent anticipation turns into our domestic chore. A minor preoccupation, but still one more thing to add to a list of major preoccupations. Minor or not, a niggle that started out as a pleasure needs watching. We didn't watch it closely enough.

And we sometimes came close to revolt.

"Why me? What about you? Sorry, you're telling them a story tonight."

"You know I haven't got any imagination."

Given half a chance, we delegated the task to someone else: a cousin, a babysitter, a visiting aunt. Someone who'd been spared until now and was charmed by the idea, but disenchanted when faced with the demands of a persnickety public:

"That's not what the grandmother says!"

We were shamefully cunning too. More than once, we tried using the story as a bargaining tool.

"If you carry on, there'll be no story tonight!"

It was a threat we rarely carried out. Shouting or withholding dessert had little or no effect. But sending them to bed without a story meant plunging their daytime into a night that was too dark and leaving them without any kind of reunion. An unbearable punishment, for them and for us.

But we certainly did threaten. Sometimes because we were tired, or tempted (though we barely acknowledged it) to use that quarter of an hour for something else, some urgent domestic matter, or just for a moment of silence . . . the chance to read ourselves.

The storyteller in us was out of steam, ready to pass the torch.

— Fifteen —

School stepped in.
Taking the future in hand.
The three Rs . . .

They were genuinely enthusiastic to begin with.

They thought it was beautiful, the way all those lines and loops and circles and bridges made letters. They couldn't get over the letters fitting together to make syllables, or the syllables stacking up to make words. And the fact that some of those words were familiar was just magic.

Maman, for example. *Maman:* three bridges, a circle, a loop, three more bridges, a second circle, another loop, and two final bridges. How do you get over the wonder of it?

Picture the scene. She gets up early. She goes out with Mom, that same *maman*, into the autumnal rain (yes, an autumnal drizzle, and the light is bad, like in a disused aquarium—let's not skimp on atmospheric drama). She makes her way to school, still warm from her bed, the taste of hot chocolate in her mouth, clinging on to that hand above her head, walking hurry-up-now quickly, two steps for every one of Mom's, schoolbag joggling on her back. And then she's at the school gates, a rushed good-bye kiss, the concrete playground with its dark chestnut trees, the first shouts of the day. . . . She might huddle in the covered area or join in right away; it depends. And then they all sit at those Lilliputian tables, still and silent. Nothing moves except the pen traveling along the narrow corridor between the lines. Tongues poking out, clumsy fingers, stiff wrists . . . Bridges, lines, loops, circles, and bridges . . . She's a thousand miles from Mom now, deep in the lonely business of making an effort, surrounded by all these other lonely beings with their tongues poking out. And now the first letters are coming together. Lines of *a*'s, lines of *m*'s, lines of *t*'s . . . (Not easy, the letter *t*, with that crossbar, but a piece of cake compared to the double revolution of *f* or the unbelievable muddle that produces the loop of a *k* . . .) But all difficulties are overcome, a step at a time, to the point where, magnetized by one another, these letters end up forming syllables . . . lines of *ma,* lines of *pa* . . . and those syllables in turn form . . .

To cut a long story short, one fine morning or afternoon, her ears still ringing with the noise of the cafeteria, she witnesses the silent hatching of a word on the white page, there in front of her: *maman.*

Of course, she'd already seen it up on the board, recognized it several times, but here in front of her, written with her own fingers . . .

Hesitant at first, she mumbles the two syllables, separately: *"Ma-man."*

And, all of a sudden: "MAMAN!"

This shout of joy marks the greatest intellectual journey there is, a sort of first step on the moon, the transition from totally arbitrary signs to the most emotionally charged meaning. Bridges, loops, circles . . . and . . . *maman!* There it is before her very eyes, but the real breakthrough takes place inside her. It's not a combination of syllables or a word or a concept; it's not *a* maman; it's *her* maman, a magical transformation that says so much more than even the most accurate photograph. And yet it's nothing more than circles, bridges, which suddenly—forever—cease being just shapes and become instead this presence, this voice, this smell, this hand, this lap, this infinity of details, this everything, so absolutely intimate and so utterly foreign from what's written there on the lines of the page, between the four walls of the classroom.

The philosopher's stone.

No more, no less.

She's just discovered the philosopher's stone.

— Sixteen —

You never get over a metamorphosis like that. You don't come back from such a voyage untouched. From now on, pleasure in reading dominates all reading. And by its very nature this pleasure, delighting as it does in alchemy, is not afraid of images, not even television images, not even when they come in daily avalanches.

And if that pleasure has been lost (if you hear people saying, "My son/my daughter/young people don't like reading"), it can't be far away.

It's hardly strayed at all.

It's easy to find again.

You just have to know where to look. Go back to certain truths that have nothing to do with the effects of modern life on young people. Truths about ourselves, people who love reading and wish to share our love with others.

– Seventeen –

Swept up in that first rush of amazement, they come back from school rather pleased with themselves. Happy even. Their ink stains are so many medals. The webs traced by their pens a badge they wear with pride.

A state of happiness that makes up for the early trials and tribulations of school life: the ridiculously long days, the demands made by the teacher, the racket in the cafeteria, the first heartbreaks . . .

They arrive, open their bags, display their achievements. They reproduce the sacred words (and if it's not *maman*, it'll be *papa*, or *bonbon*, or *chat*, or their own name).

In town, they become the voice of advertising, repeating endlessly: RENAULT, SAMARITAINE, VOLVIC, CAMARGUE . . . Words drop from the skies, colorful syllables exploding in their mouths. No brand of laundry detergent can resist their powers of decoding.

"Wa-sh-iz-whit-er. What does 'washizwhiter' mean?"

It's time for the Big Questions.

— Eighteen —

Were we too easily blinded by their enthusiasm? Did we think our children's enjoyment of words would be enough for them to master books? That learning to read happened of its own accord, like walking or talking—in other words, that it was just another part of being human? Whatever the reason, it was at this point that we put a stop to our evening reading sessions.

School was teaching them to read, and they were fired up about it. It was a turning point in their lives, a newfound independence, another first step, or so we told ourselves in our muddled way, without really articulating it. It seemed so natural to us, another stage in their seamless biological evolution.

They were "grown up" now. They could read all by themselves. They walked alone in the kingdom of signs.

At last, we could have our fifteen minutes of freedom back.

Their newfound pride did little to make us think otherwise. They slipped into bed with *Babar* wide open on their knees, frowning in fierce concentration: they were reading.

Reassured, we left their bedroom without understanding—or wanting to admit—that what a child learns first isn't the act but the gestures that accompany the act. And although it may also help them learn, this ostentatious show of reading is primarily intended to reassure them and please us.

— Nineteen —

That didn't make us bad parents. We didn't abandon our children to their fate. Not a bit; we followed their progress closely. Their teacher knew we were conscientious parents, turning up to every meeting and open to discussion.

We helped the apprentices with their homework. When they showed the first signs of running out of steam, we cheerfully made them read us their page a day out loud and understand what it meant.

Not always easy.

Giving birth to each syllable.

The meaning of the word gets lost as they try to put it back together again; as does the meaning of the sentence fragmented into so many words.

Let's go back.

Let's start again.

And again. And again.

"So, what did you just read? What does it mean?"

The worst time to ask a question like that. They're just back from school, or we're just back from work. They're at their most tired, or we're at our lowest ebb.

"You're not trying!"

Tempers, shouting, a dramatic show of giving up,

banging doors. But doggedly we insist, "Right, let's start again, from the beginning!"

And they'd go back to the beginning and start again, each word distorted by their trembling lips.

"Stop messing around!"

But they weren't. They were genuinely upset. It was an expression of their anguish at not being able to control things anymore, at not playing the part to our satisfaction. And it added to our worries far more than our impatience implied.

Because we were worried.

So we began comparing them to other children of the same age.

Quizzing our friends the So-and-Sos, whose daughter was doing very well at school and was devouring books, yes.

Were they deaf? Dyslexic, perhaps? Were they developing a block about school? Would they fall so far behind that they'd never catch up?

We saw various specialists. The audiogram came back normal. There were reassuring diagnoses from the speech therapists. The psychologists said there was nothing to worry about. . . .

So?

Lazy?

Just plain lazy?

No, they were going at their own pace, that's all, not someone else's, and not the steady rhythm of a lifetime either. Just their own pace as a learning reader. Speeding up, then suddenly slowing down, binges followed by long periods to digest everything, a thirst for making progress and a fear of disappointing . . .

But self-appointed teachers like us are always in a hurry. As Bankers of Knowledge, we lend only with interest. And we want that interest paid back. Quickly. Otherwise we start doubting ourselves.

— Twenty —

If young people don't like reading, let's not blame television or the modern world or school. Or rather, blame them all, but only after asking what *we* have done to that ideal reader since the days when we played at being both storyteller and book.

The scale of our betrayal!

The child, the narrative, and us. We formed a Trinity that was reunited every evening; now they're alone, in front of a hostile book.

The lightness of our sentences stopped them from getting bogged down; now having to mumble indecipherable letters stifles even their ability to dream.

We introduced them to vertical travel; now they're dragged down by effort.

We granted them the power to go anywhere; look at them now, trapped in their bedrooms, their classrooms, their book, in a line, in a word.

So where have all those magical characters gone? Those brothers and sisters, kings and queens? Those heroes pursued by villains, who, by asking for help, relieved the children's anxieties about their own existence? What could those characters possibly have to do with the brutally splattered ink marks we call letters? Have those demigods been reduced to this: printed signs?

41

And has the book become an object? What a strange metamorphosis. Alchemy in reverse. Their heroes—and they—suffocating in the silent thickness of the book.

And not least among the metamorphoses is Mom and Dad's newfound determination, like the teacher's, to make them explain the story that is in their head.

"So, what happened to the prince, hmm? I'm waiting!"

These same parents who never, ever worried before if their child had understood that Beauty was sleeping in the woods because she'd been pricked by a spindle. Or Snow White because she'd taken a bite out of the apple. (They hadn't really understood the first few times, as it happens. There was so much amazing stuff in those stories, so many pretty words, so much emotion. All their energy went into anticipating their favorite part and repeating it when it came around. There were other, more obscure, passages too, where the plot thickened. But gradually they understood everything, absolutely everything: they knew that if Beauty was sleeping, it was because of the spindle, and Snow White because of the apple. . . .)

"I'm asking you again: what happened to the prince when his father banished him from the castle?"

We go on and on about it. Good grief, it's unbelievable the kid hasn't understood those fifteen lines!

We used to be their storyteller. We've become their accountant.

"If that's the way you want it, there'll be no television!"

Oh, yes!

Television given the status of a reward . . . and reading reduced to a chore. Brilliant.

― Twenty-one ―

Reading is the scourge of childhood and almost the only occupation we know to prescribe. . . . A child is hardly interested in perfecting the instrument with which we torture him, but make that instrument serve his pleasures and he will soon apply himself, in spite of you.

A great to-do is made of finding the best methods for learning to read. We devise bureaux and cards, we turn the child's bedroom into a printing press. . . . What a pity! A far surer method, and the one that always gets forgotten, is the desire to read. Give the child that desire, and leave your bureaux right there . . . any method will work from then on.

To capture his interest; that's the great motive, and the only one that leads surely and far. . . .

I will just add this word as an important maxim: which is that, ordinarily, we obtain most surely and quickly that which we're in no hurry to obtain.

All right, we shouldn't listen to Rousseau, since he threw out his children with the family bathwater (an idiotic expression).

But his intervention is timely. It reminds us that the adult obsession with "knowing how to read" is nothing new. Nor are foolish teaching methods that operate counter to the desire to learn.

And (the Angel of Paradox is laughing!) a bad father might have excellent educational principles, a good teacher atrocious ones. That's just the way it is.

But if Rousseau is unacceptable, what should we make of Paul Valéry, who, though quite unconnected with the Department of Education, nevertheless made an extremely edifying speech to the young female students of the austere Légion d'Honneur school, a speech entirely respectful of that educational establishment, in which he suddenly started talking about the essence of love, love of books:

> Young ladies, Literature never first seduces us through vocabulary and syntax. Remember, quite simply, how Letters were introduced into your lives. At our most tender age, hardly do our elders stop singing the song that makes the newborn smile and sleep, than the time of tales beckons. The child drinks these stories up as if he was drinking his milk. He demands to know what happens next, and for the most wondrous passages to be repeated; he is a merciless and an excellent audience. God knows how many hours I've spent giving my little ones their fill of magicians, monsters, pirates, and fairies, as they kept crying out, "Again!" to their exhausted father.

— Twenty-two —

He is a merciless and an excellent audience.

Our children start out as good readers and will remain so if the adults around them nourish their enthusiasm instead of trying to prove themselves. If we stimulate their desire to learn before making them recite out loud; if we support them in their efforts instead of trying to catch them out; if we give up whole evenings instead of trying to save time; if we make the present come alive without threatening them with the future; if we refuse to turn a pleasure into a chore but nurture it instead. If we do all this, we ourselves will rediscover the pleasure of giving freely—because all cultural apprenticeship is free.

— Twenty-three —

That pleasure is not far away. It's easy to rediscover it. But don't let the years go by. Just wait for nightfall, open the bedroom door, sit by their bed, and start reading together again.

Reading.

Out loud.

Freely.

Their favorite stories.

It's worth describing what happens. To start with, they can't believe their ears. They've been burned by storytelling before, so they're wary. Blanket pulled up to the chin, they're on the alert, waiting for the catch. *Right, what did I just read to you? Did you understand it?*

But this time we don't ask that kind of question. Or any others either. We're just happy to read. No strings attached. They relax a bit. (So do we.) Slowly, they adopt that look of dreamy concentration, which used to be their evening face. And they recognize us at last, now that we've found our voice again. They might fall asleep after the first few minutes, from the shock, the relief.

The following evening, same reunion. Probably the same story too. Yes, the chances are they'll ask for the same story, to prove that last night wasn't a dream. They'll ask the same questions, in the same places, just for the pleasure of hearing the same answers. The repetition reassures them. It's proof of intimacy. The breath of intimacy. They need to rediscover that.

"Again!"

"Again, again . . ." really means "We must love each other, you and I, if this one story, told and retold, is all we need." Reading again isn't about repeating yourself; it's about offering fresh proof of a love that never tires.

That's why we read it again.

The day is over. We're here, together at last, somewhere else. They've rediscovered the mystery of the Trinity: them, the story, and us (in any order you like, because not being able to distinguish the different elements of this fusion is part of the fun).

Until they allow themselves the reader's ultimate pleasure, which is to grow weary of the story and ask us to move on to another one.

How many evenings are lost like this, unlocking the doors of the imagination? A few, no more. All right, maybe a few more. But it's worth it. They're open to all kinds of stories again.

Meanwhile, school perseveres with the apprenticeship. There's no need to panic if they're not making progress chanting out loud at school. Time is on our side, ever since we abandoned the idea of making up for lost time.

"Progress" will pop up somewhere else, when you're least expecting it.

One evening, when we skip a line of the story, we'll hear them shout out, "You missed a part!"

"Sorry?"

"You missed it, you've skipped a part!"

"No, I don't think so. . . ."

"Give it to me!"

They'll grab the book and point, triumphantly, to the missed line. *Which they'll read out loud.*

That's the first sign.

Others will follow. They'll develop the habit of interrupting us while we're reading.

"How d'you spell that?"

"What?"

"Prehistoric."

"P-R-E-H-I-S—"

"Show me!"

Let's not kid ourselves. This sudden curiosity is only partly because of their new vocation as alchemist; mostly it's about making the evening last as long as possible. (Making it last and last . . .)

Another time they'll say, "I'm reading with you!"

Their head on our shoulder, their eyes follow the lines we're reading for a while.

Or, another time, "I want to start!" And they'll attack the first paragraph.

Yes, all right, reading is hard work, and they're quickly out of breath. But when they've calmed down, they read fearlessly. And their reading will get better and better, the more they enjoy the experience.

"It's my turn this evening!"

The same paragraph, of course—one of the advantages of repetition. Then another, their "favorite bit." Then whole books. Books they know almost by heart, which they recognize more than read, but read all the same because they enjoy recognizing them. The time is not far off when we'll catch them, at some point during the day, with *Les contes du chat perché* on their lap, grooming the farm animals with Delphine and Marinette.

A few months ago, they were amazed to recognize *maman*. Today, a whole story emerges from the rain of words. They've become the hero of their reading sessions. The envoy appointed forevermore by the author to free the characters caught in the web of the story—so that they in turn can rescue the reader from their daily routine.

There it is. The battle's won.

And, if we want to pay them the ultimate compliment, all we have to do is nod off while they're reading to us.

~ Twenty-four ~

You'll never make a boy in the middle of a gripping story understand—you'll never get him to understand through a demonstration intended for him alone—why he must stop reading and go to bed.

It was Kafka who said that, little Franz, whose father wanted him to spend every night counting.

2
READING MATTERS

(The Dogma)

~ Twenty-five ~

But what of our teenagers, up in their bedrooms? They still need to get back on good terms with books.

The house feels empty now; their parents have gone to bed and the television's off. They're all alone . . . with page forty-eight.

And there's a book report to hand in tomorrow.

Tomorrow . . .

A quick bit of mental arithmetic:

$446 - 48 = 398.$

Three hundred and ninety-eight pages to knock off tonight. They start reading again, doggedly. One page, then another. The words dance between their headphones. Joylessly, lead-footed, falling one after another, like horses on a battlefield. Not even the drumbeat pounding in their ears can resuscitate them. They carry on reading without a backward glance at the corpses. The words have surrendered their meaning, may their letters rest in peace. Undeterred by the carnage, they read on like a soldier advancing. Impelled by a sense of duty. Page sixty-two. Page sixty-three.

They read.

Read what?

The story of Emma Bovary.

The story of a girl who read a lot.

She had read Paul et Virginie *and had dreamed of the bamboo hut, of Domingo the black man and Fidèle the dog, but above all of the sweet friendship of a dear little brother who'd pick crimson fruit for you from great trees taller than steeples, or come running barefoot over the sand to bring you a bird's nest.*

Better call Thierry or Stéphanie, ask to borrow their book report tomorrow morning, and copy it quickly before class. No one will be any the wiser. And anyway, they owe me one.

When she was thirteen, her father took her to the city, to place her in a convent. They stopped at an inn in the Saint-Gervais quarter, where at supper they had painted plates depicting the story of Mademoiselle de la Vallière. The explanatory captions, obliterated here and there by knife scratches, all glorified religion, refinement of sentiment, and the splendors of the court.

The phrase "at supper they had painted plates" raises a weary smile. "So they ate empty plates? Chewed on La Vallière's story?" They're being cheeky and deliberately missing the point, but their sarcasm is actually spot-on. There's a symmetry between their misfortunes and the ones they're reading about: Emma sees her plate as a book; they see their book as a plate.

56

~ Twenty-six ~

Meanwhile, back at school (to use the Belgian comic-strip language of their generation), the parents are on the case.

"You see, the problem with my daughter and books . . ."

The teacher understands: the student in question "doesn't like reading."

"It's surprising, really, when you think how much she read as a child. . . . She was a voracious reader. I think that's a fair description, don't you, darling?"

Darling agrees: she was a voracious reader.

"We've banned television, you know!"

(Here we go: total ban on watching TV . . . Solve a problem by forbidding it, another brilliant teaching strategy.)

"No television during the school year; it's a rule we stick to."

No television, but piano from five to six; guitar from six to seven; ballet on Wednesdays; judo, tennis, and fencing on Saturdays; cross-country skiing from the first flurry of snowflakes; sailing school from the first rays of sunshine; pottery on rainy days; trips abroad; gymnastics . . .

She won't have a moment to herself.

No time to dream.

No chance of being bored.

But being bored is *great*.

A long stretch of boredom . . . and all kinds of creativity are possible.

"We make sure she's never bored."

(Poor her.)

"We're determined—how can we put this?—to give her a *well-rounded* education. . . ."

"A *useful* education, darling—I prefer the word *useful*."

"And that's why we're here."

"Fortunately, she's doing rather well in math."

"But in French . . ."

Oh, the miserable, pathetic strain on our pride, our failure exposed as we turn up to meet the teacher. He listens, this teacher, and says, "Yes, yes," and hopes against hope that once, just once, in his long teaching career, things will be different. . . . But no, here it comes:

"Do you think she'll have to stay back a year?"

— Twenty-seven —

And so it goes: our teenagers trafficking book reports, us haunted by the specter of failure, and the French teacher feeling his subject has been devalued. . . . Let's hear it for books!

— *Twenty-eight* —

A teacher soon becomes an old teacher. The job is no more strenuous than any other, but you have to listen to so many parents talking about so many children (and talking about themselves in the process), listen to so many life stories, so many divorces and family sagas, from childhood illnesses and uncontrollable teenagers to darling daughters who now hate their parents, so many sob stories and so much boasting, so many opinions on so many different subjects. But what you hear most often is how much reading matters, how much reading *really does matter*. On that they are all agreed.

Dogma.

Some people never read and are ashamed of it. Others don't seem to have time to read anymore but keep saying how much they miss it. Some don't read novels but prefer useful books: essays, manuals, history books. Others read voraciously, devouring books with shining eyes. Some only read the classics because "they've stood the test of time," and some spend their adult life rereading. And then there are those who've always read the latest Such-and-Such by So-and-So, because, well, you've got to keep up, haven't you?

But all of them, every single one, stress how much reading matters.

Dogma.

Including the ones who'll tell you that, even if they're not reading today, it's because they read a lot yesterday. Their student days are behind them now and they've made it on their own (they're the kind who are beholden to no one), but they're happy to tell you that those books they don't read anymore were useful at the time. "Essential, in fact. Yes, *es-sen-tial!*"

"That's what kids need to get into their heads."

Dogma.

— Twenty-nine —

Well, the kids have certainly got it into their heads. They don't question the dogma, not for a second. That much at least is clear from their essays:

Subject: *What Do You Think of Gustave Flaubert's Advice to His Friend Louise Collet, "Read to Live"?*

They agree with Flaubert, and so do all their friends, male and female alike: "Flaubert was right!" Thirty-five essays, one voice: reading matters; you've got to read to live. Our need to read is what separates us from the animals, from the ignorant and brutish, from shrill sectarianism, from despots, crude materialists. . . . Reading matters! You've got to read!

"To learn."

"To do well at school."

"To be well informed."

"To understand where we come from."

"To find out who we are."

"To have a better understanding of others."

"To know where we're going."

"To preserve the past."

"To illuminate the present."

"To learn from experience."

"To avoid repeating the mistakes of the past."

"To save time."

"To escape."

"To make sense of life."

"To understand the foundations of our civilization."

"To make us want to find out more."

"To be cultured."

"To communicate."

"To develop our critical faculties."

And the teacher shows his approval in the margin. Yes. Yes. Good. Very good. Quite good. Exactly. Interesting. Absolutely. Quite right. He has to stop himself from shouting out, "More! More!" But the same teacher saw our reluctant reader furiously copying Stéphanie's book report in the corridor this morning. He knows that most of the quotations in these essays are cribbed from passed notes. He can see at a glance the examples chosen ("Give examples based on your own personal experience") are from other people's work. His ears are still ringing from the chorus of protest when he set the reading homework for their next novel.

"You what? Four hundred pages in two weeks! We'll never make it!"

"We've got a math test!"

"And an economics essay to hand in next week!"

And, even though he is aware of the role television plays in the lives of Mathieu, Leïla, Brigitte, Camel, and Cédric, he carries on showing his approval, with all the red ink left in his pen, as Cédric, Camel, Brigitte, Leïla, and Mathieu claim that TV ("Don't use abbreviations in your essays!") is Enemy Number One of books — along with movies, when you think about it — since they're both fundamentally passive, while reading involves active responsibility (Very good!).

But at this point, the teacher puts down his pen, looks up like a student daydreaming, and wonders if some films haven't, in fact, made the kind of impression on him that books have. How many times has he "reread" *The Night of the Hunter, Amarcord, Manhattan, A Room with a View, Babette's Feast,* or *Fanny and Alexander*? Images from these films seem to him loaded with symbolic language. Of course, he's no expert. He knows nothing about the syntax of cinematography and has no access to the film buff's lexicon. But he could see, with his own eyes, that the meaning of these images would never be exhausted, knew that his emotional response to them would be fresh every time. Even television: the aging face of the philosopher Gaston Bachelard, on *Lecture pour tous,* or Vladimir Jankélévitch, with his signature lock of hair, presenting *Apostrophes.* Or Papin's goal against Berlusconi's Milan . . .

But time's ticking away. He gets on with his marking. (Who can ever convey the loneliness of the long-distance marker?) A few essays later, the words start dancing before his eyes. The arguments have a habit of repeating themselves. He's getting annoyed now. His students keep parroting *reading matters, reading matters,* the endless litany of the educational establishment: *reading matters.* When every sentence proves they never read!

— Thirty —

"Why are you so worked up, darling? Your students just write what you expect them to."

"Meaning what?"

"Reading matters. Dogma. Come on, you didn't think you'd get a bunch of essays in favor of burning books, did you?"

"I expect them to unplug their headphones and actually read."

"Rubbish. You expect them to write nice essays on novels *you've* assigned, properly 'interpret' poems *you've* chosen. And when it comes to exams, you expect them to offer a close reading of the books on *your* list and write well-balanced commentaries and intelligent summaries of whatever the examiner sticks under their nose that morning. . . . But none of you—the examiner, you, their parents—are actively interested in whether or not these children read. You don't *not* want them to, either. You just want them to pass their exams, end of story. You've got enough on your plate. Mind you, Flaubert felt he had plenty on his plate too. He sent Louise back to her books, so she'd leave him in peace. So he could get on with his *Bovary* and she wouldn't go making babies behind his back. That's the truth, and you know it. What Flaubert really meant when he wrote "Read to live" to Louise was "Read to let *me* live." Did you explain that to your students? And if not, why not?"

She smiles. Puts her hand on his.

"Get used to the idea, darling. The cult of reading is rooted in oral storytelling. And you're the high priest."

– Thirty-one –

Happily, the very selection of reading matter was such that it did not really make much difference how the schoolmasters handled it: most of the stuff was a deadly bore, anyhow. Almost none of the material we had to study at school was apt to seize or enrich my fancy. Whatever literary background I possess is certainly not due to the sleepy old Wilhelms gymnasium.

The voices of the great poets fuse in my memory with the voices of those who first transmitted them to me. There are certain masterpieces of the German romantic school which I cannot reread without hearing, once again, the intonations of Mielein's swift and sonorous voice. She was wont to read aloud to us, as long as we were youngsters and it still meant an effort to us to read by ourselves. . . .

His [my father's] favorites were the Russians. He read to us The Cossacks *by Tolstoy and the strangely primitive, childlike parables of his latest period; we heard stories by Gogol and even one piece by Dostoyevsky, that uncanny farce called* A Ridiculous Tale. *. . .*

No doubt, these eventful evening hours in Father's workroom meant a stimulus, not only to our imaginations but also to our curiosity. Once you have tasted the charm and solace of great literature, you become avid for more stuff of that kind, other ridiculous tales and suggestive parables. So you begin to read by yourself.

These are the words of Klaus Mann, son of Thomas, the Magician, and of Mielein, she of the swift and sonorous voice.

— Thirty-two —

This consensus on how much reading matters is somewhat depressing. Rousseau's remarks about learning to read, Klaus Mann on how the Bavarian state taught literature, the jibes of the teacher's young wife, the moaning of today's students, all amount to the same thing. Schools everywhere have always confined themselves to making students learn techniques and write essays, while proscribing reading for pleasure. It seems to be established in perpetuity, in every part of the world, that enjoyment has no part to play in the curriculum, and that knowledge can only be the fruit of suffering.

There's a case to be made for this.

And no shortage of supporting arguments.

Schools can't be about pleasure, with all the freedom that implies. They're knowledge factories and require effort. The subjects taught are tools of consciousness, and it's the teachers' job to initiate their students in those subjects. You can't expect them to promote education for education's sake when every aspect of school life — timetables, marks, exams, ratings, courses, subject choices, departments — reinforces competitiveness and is dictated by the job market.

If a student occasionally comes across a teacher who's genuinely enthusiastic about pure mathematics and teaches it like one of the fine arts, it's down to luck, not the brilliance of the school. That teacher's enthusiasm inspires a love of their subject and turns effort into pleasure.

Human beings will always have the capacity to inspire a love of life, even when life takes the form of quadratic equations, but enthusiasm has never been part of the curriculum.

It's all about duty.

Life is elsewhere.

You learn to read at school.

But to love reading . . .

— Thirty-three —

Reading matters, reading matters . . .

But what if, instead of setting reading assignments, the teacher suddenly decided to share his or her enjoyment of reading?

Enjoy reading? What do you mean?

The question, of course, rebounds on the questioner.

For one thing, we have to admit to something that goes against all the dogma: most of the books that shaped our lives were read in a spirit of opposition. We used to read (and still do) defensively, positioning ourselves in a state of siege. If we are escaping reality, in thrall to the magic of the book, then we are escapees busy constructing ourselves, in the process of being born.

Reading is an act of resistance. Against what? Against all constraints.

Social.

Professional.

Psychological.

Emotional.

Meteorological.

Familial.

Domestic.

Tribal.

Pathological.

Financial.

Ideological.

Cultural.

Egotistical.

A well-chosen book saves you from everything, including yourself.

But, above all, we read in defiance of our own mortality.

Think of Kafka reading in spite of his father's commercial ambitions for him. Of Flannery O'Connor reading Dostoyevsky in spite of her mother's sarcasm. (*"The Idiot?* You *would* get something called *Idiot."*) Of Thibaudet reading Montaigne in the trenches of Verdun. Of Henri Mondor deep in his own personal copy of Mallarmé in black-market, occupied France, and the journalist Jean-Paul Kauffman reading *War and Peace* over and over again in his Beirut cell. Valéry descibes a patient, being operated on without anesthetic, finding "some comfort, or rather, rallying his strength and patience by reciting, between bouts of pain, a poem he was fond of." And, of course, Montesquieu (whose mishandling by teachers has resulted in so many dull essays), said, "Study has always been my sovereign remedy for disappointment, for I have never experienced a sorrow that was not relieved by an hour of reading."

In our everyday lives, a book is a refuge from the

patter of rain, the silent dazzle of the pages blocking out the rhythm of the metro, the novel a secretary stashes in her office drawer, the moment snatched by a teacher while her students work on an assignment, and the boy at the back reading on the sly, about to hand in a blank piece of paper. . . .

— Thirty-four —

What makes teaching it so difficult is that reading is ultimately a retreat into silence.

Reading as communication? Another daft joke from the pundits.

We keep quiet about what we read. Our enjoyment of a book remains a jealously guarded secret. Perhaps because there's no need to talk, or because it takes time to distill what we've read before we can say anything. Silence is our guarantee of intimacy. We might have finished reading, but we're still living the book. Just thinking about it is an excuse for not getting on with life. It protects us from the Outside World, but at the same time it is an observation post high above the surrounding countryside. We who have read keep quiet. We're quiet *because* we've read. Imagine being pounced on as soon as you've finished? "Sooooo? Was it any good? Did you understand it? Out with it!"

Sometimes, humility makes us keep quiet. Not the false modesty of the psychoanalyst but the intimate, lonely, almost painful acknowledgment that this book or that author has changed your life. Or a sudden realization leaves us speechless: how could something that turned my whole world upside down not have changed the outside world at all? How could the century have turned out like this *after* Dostoyevsky wrote *The Devils*? How could Pol Pot and the others have come along, when Piotr Verkhovensky had already been created? Or the atrocities of the gulags, when Chekhov had already written *Sakhalin Island*? Which of us saw ourselves in the white light of Kafka's works, where the grimmest facts stand out in the starkest relief? Who was listening to Walter Benjamin as the horror was unleashed? And, after it was all over, why didn't the whole world read Robert Antelme's *L'Espèce humaine,* if only to liberate Carlo Levi's Christ, stopped forever at Eboli?

Books can affect us so profoundly, and still the world is destroyed — no wonder we keep quiet.

Silence then . . .

Except for the hollow phrases of the cultural establishment.

At dinner parties where nobody's got anything to say, books become a topic of conversation. A work of fiction reduced to a conversational gambit! All those silent screams, all that stubborn perseverence, just so a fool can chat up some stuck-up cow: "You mean, you haven't read *Voyage au bout de la nuit*?"

People kill for less.

— Thirty-five —

If reading isn't about communication, it is, in the end, about sharing. But a deferred and fiercely selective kind of sharing.

If we were to go back over all the great books we read for school, because of the critics and advertising, because of friends, lovers, classmates, and even family—when they didn't lump books with education—we'd realize that, more often than not, the books we loved best we read because of the people we loved best. Perhaps precisely because affection, like the desire to read, is about preference. Love means sharing what we like with the people we like. And this sharing helps populate the

invisible citadel of our freedom. Books, like friends, inhabit us. When a person we like gives us a book, we look for them at first between the lines — for their tastes, for the reasons they thrust it into our hands, for a sign of the bond between us. But soon we're transported by the words and forget about who introduced it to us in the first place. In fact, it is the mark of a great book that we do forget.

As the years go by, however, just a mention of the title is enough to bring back memories of that person. And so some books become attached to faces again.

To be fair, it's not always a welcome face, but it can (very occasionally!) be that of a critic or teacher.

I remember Pierre Dumayet, the television presenter of *Lecture pour tous* in my childhood. The way he looked at you, his voice, his silences, all expressed his great respect for the reader I would, thanks to him, become. The same goes for the teacher whose passion for books gave him endless patience, and us the illusion of being loved. He must surely have liked us, respected us as students, to have given us his favorite books to read.

— Thirty-six —

In his biography of Georges Perros, Jean-Marie Gibbal quotes a female student from Rennes, where Perros taught.

> "*He would come in on Tuesday mornings, beaten up by the wind and cold, on his rusty blue motorbike. Hunched in his reefer jacket, with his pipe in his mouth or his hand, he would tip a saddlebag of books onto the table. And life began.*"

Fifteen years later, this amazing woman is still amazed by him, still talks about him. Smiling over her cup of coffee, she thinks back, slowly calling up her memories.

"Yes, life began. Half a ton of books, pipes, tobacco, a copy of *France Soir* or *L'Équipe,* keys, notebooks, bills, a sparkplug from his motorbike . . . Out of this mess he'd pull a book, look at us, laugh to get us in the mood, and start reading. He used to walk around as he read, one hand in his pocket, the other holding the book, stretched out slightly as if, by reading it, he was giving it to us. Everything he read was a gift. He asked for nothing in return. When someone wasn't concentrating, he would stop reading for a moment, look at the dreamer, and whistle. It wasn't a remonstrance, but a friendly way of bringing them back. He never lost sight of us. Even when he was completely engrossed in what he was reading, he would watch us from over the top of the page. His voice was clear and resonant, if slightly hushed, and it filled the classroom perfectly, as it would have done a lecture hall, a theater, or the Champ de Mars. No single word was stressed at the expense of another. Instinctively, he sized up both the space and our brains. He was an echo chamber for all books, the physical incarnation of words, the book made human. Through his voice we suddenly discovered that all this had been written for us. A discovery made after an eternity of schooling, during which our teachers had succeeded in keeping us at a respectful distance from books. So what was he doing that our other teachers weren't? Nothing. In certain respects, he even did less. But instead of drip-feeding us literature for analysis, he served it up by the brimming glassful. And we understood everything he read us. We *heard* him. There could be no more illuminating explanation of a text than his voice as he anticipated the author's intention, exposing a hidden meaning, uncovering an allusion. You couldn't fail to understand. After hearing him read Marivaux's *La double inconstance,* it was impossible to misconstrue the author's theatrical dissection as foppish wit or to view those human puppets through rose-tinted spectacles. The surgical precision of his voice led us into an operating theater; his forensic diction invited us to witness a vivisection. But he never overdid it or tried to turn Marivaux into a forerunner of de Sade. While he was reading, we felt we were watching an experiment, in which the brains of Arlequin and Silvia were being sliced down the middle.

"He taught us for an hour a week. That hour was like his saddlebag: anything could come out of it. When he left us at the end of the year, I totted them up: Shakespeare, Proust, Kafka, Vialatte, Strindberg, Kierke-gaard, Molière, Beckett, Marivaux, Valéry, Huysmans, Rilke, Bataille, Gracq, Hardellet, Cervantes, Laclos, Cioran, Chekhov, Henri Thomas, Butor . . . I'm listing them in no particular order and forgetting just as many. In ten years at school, I hadn't heard of a tenth of them!

"He talked to us about everything, read us everything, because he took it for granted that we didn't have a library in our heads. He started from scratch, assumed we knew nothing. He took us as we were, uncultured undergraduates who deserved to know. There was no question of cultural heritage or hermetic knowledge; books didn't fall out of the sky with him—he picked them up off the ground and gave them to us to read. Everything we needed was there, around us, humming with life. I remember how disappointed we were at first when he started on the big names, the ones our teachers had told us about, the few we thought we actually knew well: La Fontaine, Molière . . . But in just an hour, they stopped being academic gods and became intimate and mysterious—that is to say, essential. Perros brought authors back from the dead. Get up and walk: from Apollinaire to Zola, Brecht to Wilde, they all turned up in our class, alive and well, as if they'd just stepped out of Chez Michou, the café opposite, where we sometimes gathered for a second session. Not that he played the teacher-friend—it wasn't his style. He was just carrying on what he called his "ignorance class." In his company, culture was no longer a state religion and the café bar was as good as any lectern. Listening to him, we didn't feel we were entering a church or putting on sacred robes of knowledge. We just wanted to read. . . . As soon as he'd finished, we raided the bookshops of Rennes and Quimper. And the more we read, the less we felt we knew. Beached on the shore of our own ignorance, looking out to sea. Except that, with him, we weren't afraid of getting wet anymore. We wasted no time shivering and splashing around but dived straight into our books. I don't know how many of us became teachers. Not many, I suspect, which is perhaps a shame. Because, without us even realizing it, he left us with a strong desire to communicate. Wherever we went. Always dismissive of formal teaching, he jokingly came up with the notion of an itinerant university: 'If only we could take a stroll . . . go and look up Goethe in Weimar, rage about God with Kierkegaard's father, read Gogol's *White Nights* on the Nevsky Prospect in St. Petersburg. . . .'"

— Thirty-seven —

Reading, the resurrection of Lazarus, lifting the stone off words.

Georges Perros, *Échancrures*

— Thirty-eight —

Perros was a teacher who didn't drum knowledge into people but made a gift of what he knew. Less a teacher than a master troubadour—one of those jugglers of words who haunted the hostelries on the way to Santiago de Compostela, performing *chansons de geste* for illiterate pilgrims.

Because everything must start somewhere, each year he gathered his flock to listen to the oral origins of the novel. Like the troubadours', his voice was aimed at a public who didn't know how to read. He opened eyes. He lit lanterns. He set people off on the road to books, a pilgrimage without end or certainty, the path of human toward fellow human.

"The most important thing was that he read everything out loud to us. From the word go, he trusted in our desire to understand. . . . When someone reads aloud, they raise you to the level of the book. They *give* you reading, as a gift."

— Thirty-nine —

Instead, we readers who say we want to share our love of books all too often choose to act as commentators. As interpreters, analysts, critics, and biographers, smothering great works in pious testimonies. Victims of our proficiency, the words in books give way to our own. Rather than allowing a book's intelligence to speak through our mouths, we replace it with our own intelligence as we talk about it. Rather than acting as emissary for the book, we become guardians of the temple, boasting of its wonders in the very words that slam shut its doors: *Reading matters! Reading matters!*

— *Forty* —

Reading matters. Saying this to teenagers is asking for trouble, no matter how brilliantly you demonstrate the truth of it.

The students who discovered books through other channels will carry on reading anyway; the more intellectually curious among them will use the shining light of our explanations to guide their readings.

The most sensible of the "non-readers" will learn, like us, to talk around the book. They'll perfect the inflationary art of commentary (read ten lines, produce ten pages), the head-shrinking practice of writing book reports (skim four hundred pages, reduce them to five). They'll fish for choice quotes from one of those Idiot's Guides to deep-freeze culture, "available at all good bookshops." They'll learn to wield the scalpel of line-by-line analysis and become expert at navigating between "selected extracts." This is the way to pass your *baccalauréat*, get your degree, even qualify as a teacher . . . but it doesn't necessarily lead to a love of books.

Then there are the rest.

The students who don't read and are terrorized from an early age by the radioactive effect of meaning.

Those who think they're stupid . . .
Condemned to a life without books . . .
A life without answers . . .
And before long, without questions too.

— Forty-one —

Let's dream a dream.

It's the day of the oral exam for new French teachers, known as "the lesson."

The topic: Registers of literary consciousness in *Madame Bovary*.

The young candidate is at her desk, far below the six members of the jury, who sit, stock-still, high up on their platform. To add to the solemnity of the occasion, let's pretend it takes place in a large amphitheater at the Sorbonne. The smell of centuries and sacred wood. The profound silence of knowledge.

The hearts of a thin scattering of parents and friends beat as one to the rhythm of the young woman's fear. The young woman is far below—so her perspective is from the bottom looking up—crushed by the dread of all the things she still doesn't know.

Gentle rustlings, stifled coughs; the pre-exam eternity.

The young woman arranges her notes with trembling hands. She opens the score of her knowledge: Registers of literary consciousness in *Madame Bovary*.

The president of the jury (it's a dream, so let's give him a gown of oxblood red and make him very old, with ermine on his shoulders and a cocker spaniel wig to accentuate his granite wrinkles), the president of the jury leans over, lifts his colleague's wig, and whispers two words in his ear. The assessor (who's younger, in the pink of wisdom, same gown, same wig) gives his qualified opinion. He turns to his neighbor while the president whispers to the colleague on his left. The acquiescing extends to both ends of the table.

Registers of literary consciousness in *Madame Bovary*. Lost in her notes, panic-stricken because her ideas are suddenly all over the place, the young woman doesn't see the jury rise, step down off the platform, come toward her, surround her. . . . She lifts her eyes pensively and finds herself caught in the net of their stares. She should be frightened, but she's too busy worrying about not knowing enough. She scarcely stops to wonder why they are so close to her. She dives back into her notes. Registers of literary consciousness . . . she's lost her lesson plan. And it was so clear! What's she done with her lesson plan? Where are all the clever points she was going to make?

"Miss . . ."

The young woman is not interested in the president. She's searching, searching for her lesson plan, which has been swept away in a whirlwind of knowledge.

"Miss . . ."

She's looking for it, but she can't find it. Registers of

literary consciousness in *Madame Bovary* . . . She finds everything else, everything she knows. But not her lesson plan. Not her lesson plan.

"Miss, please . . ."

Is it because the president's hand touches her arm? (Since when did presidents of the jury put their hand on a candidate's arm?) Is it the unexpected childlike note of supplication in his voice? Is it because the assessors are starting to shift uncomfortably in their seats? (They've each brought their chair with them and are sitting around her.) Whatever it is, the young woman finally looks up.

"Please, miss, forget about the registers of consciousness. . . ."

The president and his assessors have taken off their wigs. Their hair is downy, like little children's; their eyes are wide open; they're desperate, like starving people.

"Miss . . . tell us the story of *Madame Bovary!*"

"No! No! Tell us your favorite story!"

"Yes, *The Ballad of the Sad Café*! You love Carson McCullers—tell us *The Ballad of the Sad Café*!"

"And after that you'll make us want to read *La princesse de Clèves* again, won't you?"

"Make us want to read, miss."

"Make us really want to read!"

"Tell us the story of *Adolphe*!"

"Read us *A Portrait of the Artist as a Young Man*, the chapter with the glasses!"

"Kafka! There's all sorts of crazy stuff in his *Diaries* . . ."

"Svevo! *Zeno's Conscience*!"

"Read us *Tales from the Saragossa Manuscript*!"

"Your favorite books!"

"*Ferdydurke*!"

"*A Confederacy of Dunces*!"

"Don't look at the clock; we've got plenty of time!"

"Pleeeze . . ."

"Tell us a story!"

"Miss . . ."

"Read to us!"

"*The Three Musketeers*!"

"*A Rage in Harlem*!"

"*Jules et Jim*!"

"*Charlie and the Chocolate Factory*!"

"*Le prince de Motordu*!"

"*Basile*!"

3

THE GIFT OF READING

— *Forty-two* —

Imagine a class of about thirty-five students. Not the ones carefully fast-tracked through the *grandes écoles*. No, we're talking about the rest. The ones rejected by the central *lycées* because they weren't on track for a distinction in their *baccalauréat*; in fact, they weren't on track to pass at all.

It's a new school year.

The students here are failures.

At this school.

Facing this teacher.

Failures is the word. Washed up, while their friends are safely on board high school steamers heading for "big careers." This is the human wreckage left behind by the academic tide. And here's how they describe themselves:

SURNAME, NAME, DATE OF BIRTH.

ADDITIONAL INFORMATION:

I've always been useless at math. . . . I'm not interested in languages. . . . I can't concentrate. . . . I'm no good at writing. . . . Books have too many long words in them (*sic!* Yes, *sic!*). . . . I don't understand physics. . . . I always fail spelling tests. . . . History would be OK except I can't remember dates. . . . I don't think I work hard enough. . . . Nothing makes any sense. . . . I've missed a lot of classes. . . . I like the idea of drawing, but

I've got no talent. . . . It was too difficult. . . . I've got a bad memory. . . . I never learned the basics. . . . I don't have any ideas. . . . I can't find the right words. . . .

They're finished.

That's how they see themselves.

Finished before they've even started.

Of course, they're exaggerating a bit. It's to be expected. Filling in a form about yourself is like writing a diary. Full of self-criticism, you instinctively knock yourself. And the self-accusation is a defense against any demands that might be made of you. At least school has given them the comfort of fatalism. There's no better tranquilizer than a stream of never-ending zeros in math or spelling: avoid making any progress, and you don't have to make any effort. As for "books have too many long words," who knows, perhaps you'll never have to read anything ever again.

But these teenagers don't look like their self-portraits. They don't look like dunces, with the low brows and square chins a director would choose if he were casting them from their autobiographical snapshots.

They have as many different faces as the times they live in. Black T-shirt and cowboy boots for the rocker (there's always one). Abercrombie & Fitch for Mr. Label-Conscious. Leather jacket for the Biker with No Bike, and long hair or crew cut depending on family allegiances. A girl floats around in her father's shirt, which flaps against her ripped jeans. Another is all

decked out in black like a Sicilian Widow ("This world means little to me"), while her blond neighbor is staking everything on appearances: pin-up figure, cover-girl face, perfect makeup.

They've barely outgrown measles and mumps, and now they've caught fashion instead.

And they're tall enough to eat lunch off the teacher's head! The boys are sturdy and the girls curvy.

The teacher's own adolescence is more of a blur. He was punier, brought up on postwar junk, Marshall Plan condensed milk. Like the rest of Europe, the teacher was under reconstruction at the time.

But this lot has got *reconstructed* written all over them. Their good health and fashion consciousness make them look frighteningly mature. Their hair, clothes, headphones, cell phones, the way they talk, and their self-sufficiency all give the impression they're better adapted to life than their teacher is. That they might even know a lot more. . . .

More about what?

That's the enigma in their faces. . . .

There's nothing more enigmatic than an air of maturity.

If he weren't such an old hand, the teacher might feel he'd been written out of the present tense, a bit of an old fogey. But in twenty years of teaching, he's seen enough children and teenagers, over three thousand of them. He's seen fashions come and go too; some of them have even come around again.

The only thing that never changes is the way they fill out that form. The blatant self-destruction: I'm lazy; I'm stupid; I'm useless; I've tried everything; don't waste your time; my past has no future. . . .

They don't like themselves. And they declare it with childlike conviction.

They're between two worlds but have lost contact with both. They're "trendy," of course, "cool" (and how!). But school "stresses them out," it "does their heads in." They're not kids anymore, but it's a nightmare waiting to be a grown-up. . . .

They want to be free, but they feel abandoned.

— Forty-three —

And they don't like reading, of course. Too many long words. Too many pages. In fact, too many books period.

No, they definitely don't like reading.

Or so the forest of hands would indicate when the teacher asks, "Who doesn't like reading?"

There's an element of provocation in this almost unanimous response, while the few hands that aren't raised (including the Sicilian Widow's) are indifferent.

"All right," says the teacher, "if you don't like reading . . . I'll read *to you*."

Quickly, he opens his satchel and gets out a big fat book, a doorstop, enormous, with a glossy cover. You can't imagine a more impressive book.

"Ready?"

They can't believe their ears or eyes. This guy's going to read *that* to us? It'll take all year! Everyone's confused. Tense, even. There's no such thing as a teacher who says he'll spend the whole year reading to you. Either he's bluffing or there's something funny going on. Just you wait. There'll be a vocabulary list to learn every day, endless book reports for homework. . . .

The students look at each other. Some of them get out a clean sheet of paper, just in case, and start drumming with their pens.

"No, no, I don't want you to take any notes. Just try listening—that's all."

Which then raises the problem of what to do with your body. What happens to it in a classroom without the props—the pen and the blank piece of paper? What on earth are you meant to do?

"Settle down, relax . . ."

(Relax. Yeah, right.)

Curiosity gets the better of them, and Cowboy Boots can't help asking, "Are you going to read us the whole book . . . *aloud*?"

"I don't see how else you'd be able to hear me."

A titter. But the Sicilian Widow isn't buying it. Loud enough to be heard by everybody, she mutters, "We're too old for that kind of stuff."

And it's a common enough prejudice. Particularly among those who've never really enjoyed the gift of being read to. But the ones who have know there's no age limit.

"If you still think you're too old in ten minutes' time, raise your hand and we'll do something else, all right?"

"What kind of book is it, anyway?" asks Abercrombie, in his been-there-done-that voice.

"A novel."

"What's it about?"

"Hard to say, before we've read it. Right, are you ready? No more talking. Let's start."

They listen. Skeptically, but they listen:
"Chapter one.

"In eighteenth-century France there lived a man who was one of the most gifted and abominable personages in an era that knew no lack of gifted and abominable personages. . . ."

— Forty-four —

In the period of which we speak, there reigned in the cities a stench barely conceivable to us modern men and women. The streets stank of manure, the courtyards of urine, the stairwells stank of mouldering wood and rat droppings, the kitchens of spoiled cabbage and mutton fat; the unaired parlours stank of stale dust, the bedrooms of greasy sheets, damp featherbeds, and the pungently sweet aroma of chamber-pots. The stench of sulphur rose from the chimneys, the stench of caustic lyes from the tanneries, and from the slaughterhouses came the stench of congealed blood. People stank of sweat and unwashed clothes; from their mouths came the stench of rotting teeth, from their bellies that of onions, and from their bodies, if they were no longer very young, came the stench of rancid cheese and sour milk and tumorous disease. The rivers stank, the market-places stank, the churches stank, it stank beneath the bridges and in the palaces. The peasant stank as did the priest, the apprentice as did his master's wife, the whole of the aristocracy stank, even the King himself stank, stank like a rank lion, and the Queen like an old goat, summer and winter. . . .

– Forty-five –

Thank you, dear Mr. Süskind! The stench rising from the pages of your book makes nostrils quiver and sides split. Never has *Perfume* had thirty-five more enthusiastic readers, for all their initial reluctance. When the ten minutes were up, I can assure you, the Sicilian Widow thought she was *exactly* the right age for this. And it was touching, the way she screwed up her face to keep her laughter from drowning out your prose. Abercrombie opened his eyes and his ears, and went, "Sshh! Shut up, all right?" when one of his friends couldn't contain his hilarity. Around about page thirty-two, where you compare Jean-Baptiste Grenouille, who's staying at the boardinghouse of Madame Gaillard, to a tick forever lying in ambush (you know the bit? *The lonely tick, which, wrapped up in itself, huddles in its tree, blind, deaf and dumb, and simply sniffs, sniffs all year long, for miles around, for the blood of some passing animal* . . .), yes, around the bit where we plummeted the dank depths of Jean-Baptiste Grenouille for the first time, Cowboy Boots nodded off, his head resting on his arms. The regular breathing of an honest snooze. No, no, don't wake him—there's nothing better than a good sleep after a lullaby; it's a reader's first pleasure. Cowboy Boots is a little boy again, all trusting . . . and he's not much older when the bell rings and he calls out, "Shit, I fell asleep! What happened at Madame Gaillard's?"

— Forty-six —

My thanks to you too, Márquez, Calvino, Stevenson, Dostoyevsky, Saki, Amado, Gary, Fante, Dahl, Roché, masters living and dead. Not one of my thirty-five reluctant readers waited for their teacher before finishing your books. Why put off until next week a treat you can enjoy tonight?

"So who is he, this Süskind guy?"

"Is he alive?"

"What other stuff's he done?"

"Did he write *Perfume* in French? It sounds like he did."

(Thank you, thank you, Monsieur Lortholary, and those other Pentecostal luminaries, speakers in tongues, ladies and gentlemen of translation, thank you!)

And, as the weeks go by . . .

"*Chronicle of a Death Foretold* is brilliant! And *One Hundred Years of Solitude*, what's that about?"

"Fante, he's like—wow! It's really funny, *My Dog Stupid!*"

"Romain Gary, *La vie devant soi* . . . Fantastic!"

"Roald Dahl, he's amazing, that guy! That story about the woman who murders her husband with a frozen leg of lamb and then cooks the evidence and feeds it to the cops!"

If their critical range isn't fully developed—so what? It'll come. Just let them read. It'll come. . . .

"When you think about it, *The Cloven Viscount, Dr. Jekyll and Mr. Hyde, The Picture of Dorian Gray,* they're all sort of about the same thing: good and evil, alter egos, conscience, temptation, social morality, all that kind of stuff, aren't they?"

"Yes."

"Would you call Raskolnikov a 'romantic'?"

See. It's starting to happen.

— Forty-seven —

But it's no miracle. The teacher can take almost no credit for what happens. Because this pleasure in reading was always there, hidden away in the attics of their teenage minds because of a secret fear, the (very, very deep-rooted) fear of not understanding.

Put simply, they'd forgotten what a book was, what it could offer. They'd forgotten, for example, that a novel tells a story first and foremost. They didn't know a novel is meant to be read *like a novel*: to satisfy our thirst for narrative.

They'd long ago turned to the small screen for that, which does its assembly-line job of showing cartoons, series, soaps, and thrillers back to back, in an endless chain of blurred stereotypes: our ration of fiction. It crams your head much as you cram your belly: it fills you up, but it doesn't hang around long. It's instantly digested. And you're left feeling just as lonely as you were before.

With this public reading of *Perfume*, our teenage readers found themselves face-to-face with Süskind, the author. It was a story, they were sure about that, a ripping yarn, droll and baroque at the same time, but it was also a voice, Süskind's voice (later on, in their essays, they'll call it "style"). A story, yes, but a story told *by someone*.

"The beginning's incredible. *The unaired parlours stank . . . People stank. . . . The rivers stank, the market-places stank, the churches stank . . . the King himself stank. . . .* We're always told to avoid repetition, but it sounds beautiful, doesn't it? It's funny but it's beautiful too, wouldn't you say?"

Yes, the charm of his style makes the story all the more enjoyable. After we've read the final line, it's the echo of his voice that stays with us. Even through the double filter of translation and the teacher reading aloud, Süskind's voice is not that of Márquez ("You notice it right away!") or Calvino. Hence the peculiar feeling that Süskind, Márquez, and Calvino are addressing their words to you alone. For while stereotypes speak the same language the world over, these authors speak their own language, and tell their story *just for you;* for you, the young Sicilian Widow, the Biker with No Bike, Cowboy Boots, and Abercrombie. Already they're getting to know different authorial voices and getting a taste for what they like.

Many years later, as he faced the firing squad, Colonel Aureliano Buendía was to remember that distant afternoon when his father took him to discover ice. At that time Macondo was a village of twenty adobe houses, built on the bank of a river of clear water that ran along a bed of polished stones, which were white and enormous, like prehistoric eggs.

"I know the opening line of *One Hundred Years of Solitude* by heart. With those stones, 'white and enormous, like prehistoric eggs . . .'"

(Thank you, Señor Márquez, you started a game that was to last the whole year: collecting and remembering opening sentences and favorite bits from novels we enjoyed.)

"My favorite beginning's from *Adolphe*, when he talks about being shy:

"I did not know that my father was timid, even with his son, and that often, having waited a long while for some sign of affection from me which his apparent coldness seemed to prohibit, he would leave me, his eyes moist with tears, and complain to others that I did not love him."

"Just like me and my dad!"

They used to be closed books, staring at a closed book. Now they're swimmers, let loose in its pages.

The teacher's voice has certainly helped: by sparing them the slog of code breaking, by making situations clear, establishing the setting, stressing themes, accentuating nuances, in short, by developing the photograph as cleanly as possible.

But, in no time, the teacher's voice gets in the way, interfering with a more subtle experience.

"It helps when you read to us, but afterward I like being alone with the book."

What's happened is that the teacher's voice, in making them a gift of the story, has reconciled them with writing and helped them find their silent, secret alchemist's voice again. The same alchemist who, some ten years earlier, was astounded to find that *maman* written on a piece of paper was actually Maman in real life.

The real pleasure of reading a novel is discovering your paradoxical intimacy with the author. The solitude of the writing cries out for the words to live again, silently, internally.

The teacher is just a matchmaker here. The time has come for him to tiptoe away.

— Forty-eight —

As well as the pathological fear of not understanding, students have to confront another phobia if they are to reconcile themselves to the idea of reading on their own. And that is how *long* it takes.

They regard books as never-ending.

When they saw *Perfume* being taken out of their teacher's satchel, they saw the tip of an iceberg. (I should point out that the teacher in question had deliberately chosen the Fayard edition, which has large type, lots of blank pages, and huge margins. To these reluctant readers, a big book means interminable torture.)

But as soon as he starts to read, they see the iceberg melt in his hands!

Time flies, minutes flash by in seconds. Forty pages have been read and it's the end of class.

The teacher's doing forty an hour.

Which makes 400 pages in ten hours. Based on five hours of French a week, he could read 2,400 pages in a term, 7,200 over the school year. Seven thousand-page novels. In just five hours of reading per week!

This fantastic discovery changes everything. A book doesn't take that long after all. If I read an hour a day, for a whole week, I'll get to the end of a 280-page novel. And I could read it in just three days if I spent a bit more than two hours on it. Two hundred eighty pages in three days! Or 560 in six working days. If the book's cool—"*Gone with the Wind*'s really cool"—they'll find the extra four hours on Sunday (the suburb where Cowboy Boots lives is dead on Sundays, and Abercrombie's parents always take him off to mope in the countryside), making us 160 pages better off: a total of 720 pages!

Or 540 if I read thirty pages an hour, a respectable average. Or 360 if I stroll along at twenty an hour.

"Three hundred sixty pages a week. And you?"

Count your pages, students, count them. Novelists do. You should see them when they reach page 100! Page 100 is the novelist's Cape Horn. A cork pops inside them, they do a little jig, snort like a cart horse—and there they go, diving back into their inkwells to attack page 101. (A cart horse diving into an inkwell, now there's an image!)

Count your pages. You start off being amazed at the number you've read. Then comes a moment when you're alarmed by how little is left. Only fifty pages! You'll see. There's nothing more exquisite than that sadness. *War and Peace*: two big fat volumes . . . but only fifty pages left.

You slow down, slow down, but there's nothing you can do about it. . . .

Natasha finally marries Pierre Bezukhov: The End.

─ *Forty-nine* ─

So if I've got to find time to read every day, which part of my life should I take it from? Friends? TV? Going out? Family? Evenings in? Homework?

How am I going to find the time to read?

A big problem.

Or is it?

If you're wondering how you'll find time, it means you don't really want to read. Because nobody's ever got time. Children certainly haven't, nor have teenagers or grown-ups. Life always gets in the way.

"Read? I'd like to, but what with work, the children, and the house, I haven't got time anymore . . ."

"I'm so jealous of you having time to read!"

So how is it that this woman—who works, does all the shopping, brings up the kids, drives her car, loves three men, goes regularly to the dentist, and is moving next week—has time to read? When that guy with the private income, who's single, with no responsibilities, hasn't?

Time to read is always time stolen. (Like time to write, for that matter, or time to love.)

Stolen from what?

From the tyranny of living.

Which explains why the metro (festering symbol of said tyranny) is one of the biggest libraries in the world.

By making time to read, like making time to love, we expand our time for living.

If we had to think of love in terms of our busy schedule, who'd risk it? Who's got time to fall in love? But have you ever seen someone in love not finding time for it?

I've never had time to read, but nothing's ever stopped me from finishing a novel I loved.

Reading isn't about managing your social life better; it's a way of being, like being in love.

The question isn't whether I have time to read or not (time that nobody will ever give me, by the way), but whether I'll allow myself the pleasure of being a reader.

Cowboy Boots sums it up with a snappy slogan: "Time to read? It's in my pocket!"

And when he sees what Cowboy Boots is getting out of his pocket (*Legends of the Fall* by Jim Harrison), Abercrombie agrees. "Yes, when you buy a jacket, it's important the pockets are big enough for a paperback!"

— *Fifty* —

In French slang we talk about being "tied to" a book.
Figuratively speaking, a big book is a "brick."
Untie yourself, and the brick becomes a cloud.

— Fifty-one —

As a teacher, you will only patch up your students' relationship with reading on one condition: that you ask for nothing in return. Nothing. Don't bombard them with information. Don't ask any questions. Don't add a single word to what you've read. No value judgments, no glossing the meaning of difficult words, no textual analysis, no biographical information. Ban any talking around the subject.

Reading as a gift.

Read and wait.

Curiosity is awakened, not forced.

Read, read, and have faith that eyes will open, faces light up, that a question will be born and lead to more questions.

If the teacher in you is unhappy about not presenting the work in context, then you need to convince yourself as a teacher that, for now, the only context that counts is this class.

The road to knowledge doesn't lead into this class-room: it leads *out* of it.

For now, I read novels to an audience convinced they don't like reading. I can't teach my students anything serious until I've dispelled that illusion and done my work as matchmaker.

As soon as these teenagers are back on good terms with books, they'll happily go down the path that leads from the novel to its author, from the author to his or her time, from received history to myriad interpretations.

What matters is that you're ready.

Waiting, steadily, for the deluge of questions.

"This Stevenson guy, was he English?"

"Scottish."

"What period?"

"Nineteenth century, during the reign of Queen Victoria."

"Wasn't she queen for a long time?

"Sixty-four years: 1837 to 1901."

"Sixty-four years!"

"She'd already been on the throne for thirteen years when Stevenson was born, and he died seven years before her. So if you're fifteen today, and she comes to the throne, you'd be seventy-nine at the end of her reign! (At a time when the average age was thirty.) And she wasn't exactly a laugh, as queens go."

"That's why Hyde was born out of a nightmare."

The Sicilian Widow has spoken. Abercrombie is stunned.

"How d'you know that?"

The Sicilian Widow plays hard to get.

"I have my sources. . . ."

Then, conceding the glimmer of a smile, "And I'll tell you another thing: he had fun with the nightmare. When he woke up, Stevenson locked himself in his study for two days and drafted the first version of the book. His wife made him burn it right away, because he was just a bit too comfortable in Hyde's skin: pillaging, raping, slitting the throat of everything that moved. Not something that fat queen would have liked. So he invented Jekyll."

— Fifty-two —

But reading aloud isn't enough. You've got to tell the story, make a gift of your treasures, unwrap them for your uninitiated audience. Oyez! Oyez! Come and hear what a beautiful thing a story can be!

There's no better way to tempt a reader's appetite than by excess.

When she was talking about Georges Perros, that amazed student said, "Reading wasn't enough for him. He told us stories! He told us the story of *Don Quixote*, of *Madame Bovary*! Vast chunks of critical intelligence, but served up to us, in the first place, as simple tales. From his lips came Sancho, a wineskin of life, and the Knight of the Sorrowful Countenance, a bag of bones armed with diabolically painful convictions. Emma wasn't just a fool who got gangrene from spending too much time in "the dust of old lending libraries," but a creature with phenomenal energy. And it was Flaubert we heard, through Perros's voice, scoffing at what an enooormous mess she was!"

Dear librarians, guardians of the temple, I'm glad all the books in the world have found a place in your perfectly organized memories. (How would I find my way around without you, when my own memory's so patchy?) And I'm astounded by your knowledge of all the subjects on your stacks. But it would be good to hear you *tell* your favorite novels to visitors lost in the forest of what-to-read-next. What a great thing if you paid tribute to your favorite reads! Be storytellers—magicians—and the books will jump straight off the shelves and into the reader's hands.

Telling a story is so simple. Sometimes, three words will do.

A childhood memory: It's summer, siesta time. Big brother's lying on his bed, chin propped in his hands, absorbed in an enormous paperback. Little brother's pestering him, like a fly that won't buzz off.

Little Brother: "What are you reading?"
Big Brother: "*The Rains Came.*"
Little Brother: "Is it good?"
Big Brother: "Damn good!"
Little Brother: "What's it about?"
Big Brother: "A guy who drinks lots of whiskey to start with and lots of water by the end."

That's all it took—I spent the rest of that summer soaked to the skin by Louis Bromfield's *The Rains Came,* stolen from my brother, who never got to finish it.

— *Fifty-three* —

Now Süskind, Stevenson, Márquez, Dostoyevsky, Fante, Chester Himes, Lagerlöf, and Calvino are all very well. So many novels read in no particular order, and nothing asked in return. So many stories told in a sort of anarchic book feast, purely for the pleasure of reading. But the curriculum, good God, the curriculum! The weeks go by and we still haven't started it. Terrifying—the year slipping by, the specter of that unfinished curriculum haunting us. . . .

Don't panic—the syllabus will be covered.

Contrary to Cowboy Boots's expectations, the teacher won't be spending the whole year reading. Alas, alack! Why are his students so quick to feel the need to read silently, by themselves? Scarcely has the teacher started reading a novel aloud than they rush to the bookshop to get the next installment before the following class. Scarcely has he told two or three stories—"Not the end, don't tell us the end!"—before they're devouring the books they came from.

(But he shouldn't be fooled by their enthusiasm. A wave of his wand has not transformed reluctant readers into bookworms—everyone reads at the start of the school year, once they've conquered their fear. Of course they do. They read enthusiastically, in copycat fashion.

Perhaps they even read to try to please the teacher, whether he likes it or not. All the more reason why he shouldn't fall asleep over burning coals. Nothing goes cold more quickly than passion, as he knows from experience. But for now they're all reading together, under the influence of that magic that turns a class into a single reading being, while keeping its thirty personalities distinct. This isn't to say that, once they've grown up, all of these students will love reading. Other pleasures may predominate. But in the first few weeks of the school year, nobody is traumatized by the act of reading—reading as something you *do*. They read, and sometimes very quickly.)

What is it about these novels that means they can be read so quickly? Are they easy to read? What does "easy to read" mean? Is it easy to read *Gösta Berling's Saga*? Is it easy to read *Crime and Punishment*? Easier than *The Stranger* or *The Red and the Black*? No, but they're not on the syllabus. This is a huge advantage for the Sicilian Widow and company, who instantly brand any book selected by the powers that be to broaden their cultural horizons as "booooring." Poor old syllabus, it's not its fault. (Rabelais, Montaigne, La Bruyère, Montesquieu, Verlaine, Flaubert, Camus—booooring? You must be joking!) Fear is what makes set texts booooring. Fear of not understanding, fear of giving the wrong answer, fear of someone peering over your shoulder, fear of opaque language. There's nothing like fear for making the lines blur, for drowning out the meaning at the heart of a sentence.

Abercrombie and Biker are the first to be surprised when the teacher tells them that Salinger's *Catcher in the Rye*, which they've just raced through, is making their fellow students in the United States miserable simply because it's on the syllabus, and there might be a Texan Biker enjoying *Madame Bovary* on the sly while his teacher wears herself out trying to flog him with Salinger!

A comment from the Sicilian Widow: "Texans don't read."

"Really? And where did you get that idea from?"

"*Dallas*. Have you ever seen anyone on *Dallas* reading a book?"

By traveling from book to book, by journeying without a passport among the works of foreign writers (foreign writers above all — English, Italian, Russian, and American authors have the cachet of being far removed from the syllabus), the students are reconciled to the idea of enjoying reading and close in, in ever-smaller circles, on the set texts. And soon they dive in effortlessly, for the simple reason that *La princesse de Clèves* is now a novel like any other, and just as fun to read. (This story of a love safeguarded from love is curiously appealing to today's teenagers, for all we claim that they're slaves to the idea of sex.)

Dear Madame de Lafayette,
In case you're interested, I know an eleventh-grade class with
a reputation for being "unruly" rather than "literary," who
voted your Princesse de Clèves Best Read of the Year.

So the syllabus will get covered: essay-writing techniques, textual analysis (how methodical those academic drills are), commentary, summary, and discussion will be duly taught. The cogs of the machine are oiled to perfection so that, on exam day, the students can make clear to the relevant authorities that they don't read just for fun but that they've actually made an effort to understand.

The question of what they've understood (the final question) isn't without interest. Have they understood the text? Yes, yes, of course. But what they've understood above all is that once you've come to terms with the idea of reading, and the text is no longer a paralyzing enigma, then the struggle to find its meaning becomes a pleasure. The fear of not understanding overcome, effort and pleasure work powerfully in tandem. The more I try, the more I enjoy; and the more I enjoy, the more I want to try.

The students have understood something else too. With some amusement, they realize they've understood "how the system works," how to "talk around" a subject, how to sell themselves in the marketplace of exams. No point denying it—this is one of the goals. As far as exams and job interviews go, "understanding" means understanding what's expected of us. A book that's been "well understood" is a book that has been intelligently negotiated. The payoff is in the examiner's face when the young candidate glances sneakily up at him after giving a clever—but not too clever—interpretation of a famously enigmatic alexandrine. (He looks pleased; I'll carry on like this; it'll get me an A.)

Looked at from this point of view, a proper literary education is as much about strategy as about a genuine understanding of the text. And a bad student is, more often than you might think, a kid tragically short of tactics. The students, alarmed by their own inability to give us what we want, are quick to confuse "being a good student" with being cultured. School has washed its hands of them, and they soon feel like outcasts from the world of reading. They imagine it's elitist and deprive themselves of books all their lives, just because they didn't know how to talk about them when they were asked to.

There's still something to be understood here.

— Fifty-four —

What we need to understand is that books weren't written so that young people could write essays about them, but so that they could read them if they really wanted to.

Knowledge, academic track record, career, and social life are one thing. Our intimacy and cultural awareness as readers are quite another. It's all very well churning out qualified graduates, fast-track teachers, and high-flying civil servants—society will always have a need for them, no doubt about it. But it's much more important to make every page of every book available to everyone.

From elementary school to high school, students are made to annotate and comment, using methods that scare the majority so much they avoid books altogether. The zeitgeist doesn't help either. Commentary rules to such an extent that the text we are writing about is obscured from view. And we call the deafening chatter that results *communication*.

Telling teenagers about a book and insisting they talk about it may seem very "useful," but it's not an end in itself. The end is the book—the book they're holding in their hands. And one of their rights as readers is the right to be quiet.

— Fifty-five —

At the beginning of the school year, I sometimes ask my students to describe a library. Not a public library, but the piece of furniture where they put their books. And what they describe is a wall. A cliff of knowledge, strictly ordered, an impenetrable rock face.

"And a reader? Describe a reader to me."

"A proper reader?"

"If you like, although I'm not sure what 'a proper reader' means."

The more respectful among them describe God the Father: a sort of antediluvian hermit, sitting for all eternity on a mountain of books he's sucked the meaning out of so he understands the whys and wherefores of everything. Others sketch someone profoundly autistic, so absorbed by books that she is forever bumping into life's doors. Yet others paint a portrait in relief, listing everything a reader is *not*: not sporty, not lively, not funny, doesn't like food, clothes, cars, TV, music, friends. . . . And yet others, maybe more strategically, present the reader as an academic, someone for whom books are resources that increase access to knowledge and refine meaning. Some muddle these different images together. But not one, not a single one, describes themselves, or someone in their family, or one of the countless readers they see every day on the metro.

When I ask them to describe a book for me, a UFO lands in the classroom: a mysterious object that almost defies description. Deceptively simple to look at but with multiple functions. A foreign body with all sorts of powers and dangers. A sacred object, infinitely cherished and respected, placed with priest-like solemnity on the shelves of a spotless library, and worshipped by an adoring sect with enigmatic expressions.

The Holy Grail.

Right.

Let's try debunking this vision we've planted in their heads and replace it with a more realistic account of how we book lovers treat books.

— Fifty-six —

Few objects inspire the feeling of absolute ownership that books do. Once in our hands, they become our slaves— yes, slaves, but slaves that nobody would think of setting free, because they're made of dead trees. Like slaves, they're treated appallingly, the objects of our wildest passions and most abominable rages. . . .

I fold down the corners of your pages (the dog-eared page, such a sad sight—*but I don't want to lose my place!*). I put my coffee cup on your cover, leave stains, toast crumbs, and suntan lotion smears. I cover you with thumbprints, using the thumb that stuffs my pipe while I'm reading. There's that poor Pléiade edition drying out on the radiator after it fell in the bath (*your* bath, darling, but *my* Swift!). I scrawl notes (illegible, luckily) in the margins and leave paragraphs glowing with highlighter. I cripple one book by leaving it open facedown for a week, while supposedly protecting another with a hideous reflective plastic cover. My bed's disappearing under an ice floe of books, strewn like dead birds; there's a pile of Folio paperbacks abandoned to the mildew of the attic. All those unfortunate childhood leftovers no one reads anymore are exiled to a vacation home no one goes to anymore. And the rest are now on secondhand stalls, sold cut-rate to the slave dealers. . . .

We subject books to anything and everything. It's only other people mistreating them that bothers us.

Not so long ago, I saw a woman hurl an enormous novel out the window of a speeding car. She'd paid so much for it, trusting the so-called critics, only to be bitterly disappointed. The grandfather of novelist Tonino Benacquista actually *smoked* Plato! A prisoner of war somewhere in Albania, with a scrap of tobacco in his pocket, a copy of *Cratylus* (Whatever was *that* doing there?), a match, and—presto!—a new way of having a dialogue with Socrates . . . smoke signals.

Another, more tragic, consequence of the same war: Alberto Moravia and Elsa Morante, who were forced to hide out for several months in a shepherd's hut, managed to save only two books: the Bible and *The Brothers Karamazov*. A dreadful dilemma: which of these colossi to use as toilet paper? Tough though it may be, a choice is a choice. And, death in their souls, choose they did. . . .

For all the reverence surrounding books, no living soul could prevent Spanish writer Manuel Vázquez Montalbán's hero, Pepe Carvalho, from lighting a roaring fire every night using the pages of his favorite books.

It's the price of love, of intimacy.

As soon as the book is in our hands, it belongs to us, in exactly the way children say "That's *my* book." It becomes an extension of ourselves—perhaps that's why it's so difficult to give borrowed books back. Not stealing exactly (oh, no, we're not thieves, not us)—let's just call it property changing hands or, better still, a transfer of the material. What belonged to another person when they were reading it becomes mine now that I am reading it. And the more I like what I've read, the more difficult it is to give it back to its owner.

I'm talking here about how we lay readers treat books. But the professionals aren't much better. They guillotine the paper so the words nearly touch the edge to make their paperbacks more profitable (text with no margins, letters suffocated). Or blow up a tiny novella like a balloon to con readers into thinking they're getting their money's worth (the text looks lost, whole sentences flabbergasted by such an expanse of white). Or slap on look-at-me-now jackets, with garish colors and outsize titles that scream "Read me! Read me!" Or print book-club editions on spongy paper with covers like billboards, splashed with trashy illustrations. Or set fake leather glowing in an orgy of gold foil on the pretext of publishing "deluxe" editions. . . .

In a hyper-consumerist society, books are treated in much the same way as hormone-fed chickens, and with less deference than we give nuclear missiles. Nor is the hormone-stuffed chicken a gratuitous analogy, when applied to the millions of opportunistic books written in the space of a week because, that week, the queen kicked the bucket or the president fell from power.

Seen in this light, the book is just a product, and as ephemeral as all consumer products; instantly pulped if it doesn't take off, it frequently dies without ever being read.

And as for how universities treat books, we could ask an author's opinion. Here's what Flannery O'Connor wrote on the subject, the day she found out students were being made to study her work as set texts:

> *If teachers are in the habit of approaching a story as if it were a research problem for which any answer is believable so long as it is not obvious, then I think students will never learn to enjoy fiction.*

— *Fifty-seven* —

Enough about the book.

Let's move on to the reader.

Because even more instructive than the way we treat books is the way we read them.

When it comes to reading, we grant ourselves all kinds of rights, starting with the ones we deny the young people we want to initiate into the world of books.

1. The right not to read.
2. The right to skip.
3. The right not to finish a book.
4. The right to read it again.
5. The right to read anything.
6. The right to mistake a book for real life.
7. The right to read anywhere.
8. The right to dip in.
9. The right to read out loud.
10. The right to be quiet.

For the sake of argument, I've kept them to ten. First, because it's a nice round figure, and second, because it's the number of the Commandments, and it's gratifying, for once, to see them used to authorize rather than prohibit. For if we want young people to read, we must grant them the rights we grant ourselves.

4
THE RIGHTS OF THE READER

1. *The Right Not to Read*

As with every self-respecting declaration of rights, the rights of the reader should begin with the right "not to"—in this instance, the right not to read. Otherwise, it's not a bill of rights but a pernicious trap.

Most readers exercise the right not to read on a daily basis. Given the choice between a good book and a bad TV show, the latter wins out more often than we care to admit. Nor do we read all the time. Bouts of reading are often punctuated by long periods of abstinence, when we get indigestion just looking at a book.

But that's not what's at stake here.

We are surrounded by a number of highly respectable people, some with university degrees, some of them "eminent," some even with very impressively stocked bookshelves of their own, who don't read. Or so rarely, you'd never think of giving them a

book. It could be they don't feel the need for books. Or they're too busy doing something else.

(Which amounts to the same thing, since it means they're preoccupied or obsessed with something else.) Perhaps they're experiencing another all-consuming love. These people don't like reading. It's not that you want to spend less time with them or that you don't relish their company. (At least they won't ask your opinion of what you've just read, pour scorn on your favorite novelist, or write you off as an idiot for not rushing out and buying the latest Such-and-Such, just out from This-or-That Publisher, which Mr. Big-Mouth Critic has given a rave review.) They're every bit as human as we are, as sensitive to the terrible things happening in the world, as concerned about human rights and committed to respecting them in their own fields. All of which amounts to a great deal. But—and here you have it—they don't read. That's their prerogative.

Generally speaking, the idea that reading "humanizes" us is right and good, bar a few depressing exceptions. There's no denying that you're a little more human, meaning a little more supportive of your fellow beings (less dog-eat-dog), after reading Chekhov than before.

We should be wary of trotting out the reverse logic— that anyone who doesn't read is automatically a monster in the making, or a social misfit and outcast. Otherwise, you turn reading into a moral obligation, and in no time this slippery slope has you judging the "morality" of the books themselves according to criteria that violate another inalienable right: the freedom to create. At this point, "readers" though we may be, *we* become the monsters. And God knows there are enough monsters in this world.

In other words, the freedom to write has nothing to do with the obligation to read.

What our duty as educators really amounts to is teaching children to read by introducing them to the world of literature and providing them with the means to judge freely whether they feel a need for books or not. Because, while it's fine for someone to reject reading, it's totally unacceptable that they should be—or feel that they have been—rejected *by* reading.

To be excluded from books, even the ones you can do without, is terribly sad: a solitude within solitude.

2. The Right to Skip

I read *War and Peace* for the first time when I was twelve or thirteen. It was summer vacation, and I'd seen my brother (the same brother who'd been reading *The Rains Came*) getting stuck in this enormous novel. His eyes had the faraway look of an explorer who'd stopped feeling homesick long ago.

"Is it good?"

"It's fantastic!"

"What's it about?"

"It's the story of a girl who loves one guy but marries a third."

My brother's always been good at summarizing. If only publishers would employ him to write their cover blurbs (those pathetic attempts at urging us to read stuck on the backs of books), he'd spare us all a lot of pointless sales talk.

"Will you lend it to me?"

"I'll give it to you."

I was at boarding school at the time, so his present was priceless. Two fat volumes to keep me warm all term. Five years older than me and no fool even then, he knew that *War and Peace* could never be reduced to a love story, no matter how finely crafted. But he also knew my taste for burning emotions, and he knew his enigmatic summary would arouse my curiosity. (A real teacher, to my mind.) I'm sure it was the mathematical quirkiness of his sentence that made me temporarily trade in my Bibliothèque Verte, Rouge et Or, as well as my Signes de Piste, and throw myself into *War and Peace*. "A girl who loves one guy but marries a third . . ." How could anyone resist? As it turned out, I was not disappointed, even if my brother did get his numbers wrong. Because, you see, there were four of us in love with Natasha: Prince Andrei, that rogue Anatole (but can you call what he felt love?), Pierre Bezukhov, and me. I never stood a chance, so I had to identify with the others. (But not with that total bastard, Anatole.)

Reading was even more thrilling because the story unfolded by night, by flashlight, under my tent-like covers, in the middle of a dormitory of fifty dreamers, snorers, and wrigglers. The monitor's night-light glowed close by, but so what—it's all or nothing in love. I can still feel the weight of those thick volumes in my hands. It was a paperback edition, with Audrey Hepburn's pretty face on the cover, being eyed up by a princely Mel Ferrer, with his heavy, predatory lover's eyelids. I skipped three-quarters of the book, just to follow the affairs of Natasha's heart. That said, I did feel sorry for Anatole when they amputated his leg, and I cursed that monster of a prince Andrei for staying on his feet when the cannonball was hurtling toward him at the Battle of Borodino ("Get down, for God's sake, it's going to explode! You can't do that to her—she loves you!"). I wanted to know about love and battles, and I skipped anything to do with politics or strategy. Clausewitz's theories went straight over my head, completely passed me by, but I paid very close attention to the marital problems of Pierre Bezukhov and his wife, Elena (she was a nasty piece of work, Elena, a really nasty piece of work). And when Tolstoy ranted on about Mother Russia's agrarian problems, I just left him to it.

In other words, I skipped.

It's what all children should do.

It means they can tuck in, from the earliest age, to nearly all those treasures supposedly out of their reach.

If they want to read *Moby-Dick* but are put off by Melville's explanations of whale-hunting equipment and techniques, they mustn't give up on the book but skip instead. Skip those pages and, without bothering about the rest, follow Ahab as he pursues his great white reason for living and dying. If they want to get to know Ivan, Dmitri, and Alyosha Karamazov, as well as their incredible father, let them read *The Brothers Karamazov*—it's for them, even if they've got to skip the evidence of Father Zosima or the tale of the Grand Inquisitor.

If children can't decide what they're capable of reading by choosing which bits to skip, then the great danger is that other people will do it for them, and, armed with the outsize scissors of imbeciles, they'll lop off everything they decide is too difficult. The results are ghastly. *Moby-Dick* and *Les Misérables* reduced to 150-page summaries, mutilated, stunted, mummified, rewritten in some kind of bare-bones language thought to be for young people. It's like me making it my business to redraw *Guernica* on the basis that Picasso put in too many brushstrokes for a twelve- or thirteen-year-old eye.

Even when we're grown up, and though we may be reluctant to admit it, we still skip from time to time, for reasons that are strictly between us and the book. Sometimes we deny ourselves the right to skip and read every last word, finding the author a bit long-winded here, a bit over the top there, repetitive in one place and fatuous in another. But whatever we find to say about the book, it was our choice to read it and to be annoyed. Far from being a duty, this is one of the joys of being a reader.

3. *The Right Not to Finish a Book*

There are thirty-six thousand reasons for not finishing a book: you've been there before, the story doesn't grab you, you don't see eye to eye with the author, the style gets up your nose, the absence of a distinctive voice to keep you reading. . . . It's pointless listing the thirty-five thousand nine hundred and ninety-five others, including having a toothache, a bullying boss, or a broken heart that's knocked you sideways.

So the book falls from your hands?

Well, let it fall.

We're not all like Montesquieu, instantly able to derive an hour's comfort from a good book.

But among our reasons for giving up on a book, one is worthy of further attention: the feeling of defeat. I open it, I read, and before I know it, I'm overwhelmed by something stronger than me. I reengage my brain, battle with the words. Nothing doing. No matter how sure I am this book is worth reading, I'm making no headway—or so little it doesn't count. It feels alien to me. I can't find a way in.

I let it fall.

Or rather, I put it to one side. Put it back on the shelf, with the vague intention of returning to it one day.

Andrey Biely's *St. Petersburg*, Joyce's *Ulysses*, Malcolm Lowry's *Under the Volcano*, all waited a few years for me. Others are still waiting; I'll probably never catch up with some of them. There's no point in making a great fuss. It's just the way it is.

The notion of maturity is a strange one, in relation to books. Until we reach a certain age, we're not ready for some books. Unlike fine wine, however, good books don't need to mature. They wait patiently on our bookshelves while we get old. When we think we're ready to read them, we have another stab. It can go either way: a genuine encounter or another fiasco. Perhaps we'll try again, perhaps not. But one thing's for sure: it's not Thomas Mann's fault if I haven't yet reached the top of his *Magic Mountain*.

The great novel that resists us isn't necessarily more *difficult* than another. But a chemical reaction fails to take place between its bulk and our readiness to understand it. One day, we "get" Borges, whose work has remained distant till now. But we might be a stranger to Musil all our lives. . . .

So we have a choice: either we say it's our fault, something's missing in our brain, we're just plain thick, beyond help, or we decide to go à la carte, explore the—admittedly controversial—idea of taste, and draw up our own menu of what we do and don't like.

It's sensible to recommend this latter course of action to our children. Especially as it sometimes brings with it the rare satisfaction of reading something again and finally understanding why you don't like it. And the rare satisfaction of not caring when some prig bellows in your ear, "Hoooww can you not like Stendhaaaal?"

You just can.

4. The Right to Read It Again

Going back to a book that rejected me the first time around, reading it again without skipping, reading it from a different point of view, reading it one more time just to check . . . yes, we have all these rights.

But, above all, we have the right to read a book again just for the sake of it, for the pleasure of experiencing it all over again, the joy of being reunited with it, to test how close to it we really were.

"Again, again!" we cried as children. As adults, the urge to read a book again stems from the same desire: to be enchanted by something that never changes and to find fresh wonders each time.

5. The Right to Read Anything

Speaking of taste, some of my students agonize over the classic essay question "Is There Such a Thing as a Good or Bad Book?" Often there lurks a gentle soul behind their don't-mess-with-me looks. Which explains why, instead of tackling the question from a literary point of view, they approach it ethically and want to discuss freedom of speech. So their collective response can be summed up as follows: "Of course not, everyone's free to write whatever they like, and there are as many different reading tastes as there are people." All very worthy, of course . . .

But the fact of the matter is that there *are* good novels and bad ones. Names can be named and evidence given.

Put simply, let's suppose there's something I'll call "industrial literature," which reproduces ad infinitum the same stories, manufacturing stereotypes and turning noble sentiments and powerful emotions into big business. Let's pretend it works by jumping opportunistically on events and turning them into fiction, using market research to deliver a "product" designed to excite a specific category of reader.

These are what I call "bad" novels.

Why? Because they're not about creating something new but about reproducing existing forms. Because they trade in simplification (in other words, lies), whereas the novel is the art of telling the truth (in other words, complexity). Because in flattering our reflexes, they dull our curiosity. Finally, and most important, because *there is no author,* and the reality they claim to describe doesn't exist.

This is a literature of quick fixes and cheap thrills cast in a mold and trying to make us fit that mold.

But don't think for a moment that this is a recent phenomenon, linked to the industrialization of the book. Far from it. Sensationalism, disposable wit, and cheap thrills are nothing new. To give just two examples, the old tales of chivalry got bogged down in this way, as did the romantic novel much later on. But every cloud has a silver lining, and the reaction against such literary depravity provided us with two of the finest novels the world has ever seen: *Don Quixote* and *Madame Bovary.*

So, there are good and bad novels.

Generally, we encounter the bad novels first.

And when it was my turn, I for one thought they were really good. I was lucky: no one teased me; no one rolled their eyes in despair; no one called me a fool. They just left a

few good books lying around, resisting the urge to ban the others.

A wise move.

For a while, we read good and bad books side by side. Just as we don't give up our childhood reading habits from one day to the next. Everything gets jumbled up. You emerge from *War and Peace* to dive back into the Bibliothèque Verte. You go from stories about handsome doctors and deserving nurses to Boris Pasternak and *Doctor Zhivago*—another handsome doctor, as it happens, and Lara, a deserving nurse if ever there was one.

And then, one day, Pasternak triumphs. Without even realizing it, we want to keep company with good books. We seek out writers and writing styles. We don't just want friends to play with anymore; we're looking for life companions. The anecdote by itself is no longer enough. The time has come when we ask for something else from the novel, not just the instant and total gratification of our senses.

One of the great joys of being a teacher—as long as all books are allowed—is to see a student slam the door of the Bestseller Factory and climb up to breathe the same air as their friend Balzac.

6. The Right to Mistake a Book for Real Life

(A Textually Transmitted Disease)

There's a kind of reading that is all about the instant and total gratification of the senses. Your imagination swells, nerves quiver, heart races; you get an adrenaline rush; you identify with anything and everything, as your brain momentarily loses the ability to distinguish between the world of the novel and reality.

For all of us, this is our first reading state.

Divine.

But it can be mildly alarming for the adult observer who, on seeing the impressionable young reader devouring trash, hurries to wave a "good book" under their nose, saying, "You'll get so much more out of Maupassant!"

Don't overreact.

Remember: the greatest exponent of instant gratification, Emma Bovary, is herself a character in a novel. So, not only is she a figment of Gustave Flaubert's imagination, but so too are the dire consequences of her actions, real as they may seem.

Put another way, the fact that my daughter collects Harlequin books doesn't mean she'll end up swallowing a load of arsenic.

To direct her too much at such an early stage in her reading life is to turn our backs on our own adolescence. It also means denying her the pleasure of banishing tomorrow the stereotypes she overidentifies with today.

It makes sense to be honest about our own adolescence: to loathe, despise, deny, or simply forget how we used to be as teenagers is in itself teenage behavior, based on the notion of adolescence as a deadly disease. Which is why we need to recall our first excitement as readers and enshrine in our memories the books we used to read, even the trashiest. They play a crucial role in reminding us of who we were, by making us laugh at what moved us. The children who share our lives can only gain from our increased respect and sensitivity.

It's also important to remember that this kind of instant and emotional response, when we mistake the world of a book for real life, is an almost universal experience, and one we're quicker to notice in others. So, while we complain about the ghastly reading tastes of teenagers, the chances are we ourselves are contributing to the success of the latest telegenic author we'll write off as soon as their fifteen minutes are up. In the clear light of day, infatuation gives way to rejection.

Convinced that nobody can make a fool out of us, that we're always self-aware, we spend our time reinventing ourselves, projecting ourselves anew, in the firm belief that Madame Bovary is someone else. Emma would have done the same.

7. The Right to Read Anywhere

Châlons-sur-Marne, winter 1971.

The barracks of the Applied Artillery School.

At the allocation of morning chores, Private So-and-So (matriculation number 14672/1, well known to this department) systematically volunteers for the least popular, most thankless task, which is commonly assigned as a punishment, guaranteed to ruin even the best reputation: the legendary, infamous, unspeakable "shit-house duty."

Every morning.

With the same smile (to himself).

"Shit-house duty?"

He takes one step forward.

"Private So-and-So, sir!"

With all the seriousness of somebody about to launch an attack, he grabs the broom, with the floor cloth dangling from it like the company flag, and disappears, to the great relief of the rest of the troop. Brave man; nobody follows him. The rest of the army is stuck in the trench of honorable chores.

The hours go by. Perhaps he got lost? They've almost forgotten about him. They do forget him. But he reappears at the end of the morning, clicking his heels to report to the company warrant officer, "Latrines spotless, sir!"

The warrant officer recovers the floor cloth and broom, a question in his eye that he'll never ask. (Human decency prevents him.) The soldier salutes him, turns on his heels, and withdraws, taking his secret with him.

That secret, tucked in the right pocket of his fatigues, weighs a ton: 1,900 pages of the complete works of Nikolai Gogol, the Pléiade edition. A quarter of an hour with the floor cloth in exchange for a morning with Gogol. Each winter morning, for the past two months, ensconced in the throne room (double-locked), Private So-and-So has soared above military routine.

All of Gogol! From the nostalgic *Evenings on a Farm Near Dikanka* to the hilarious Petersburg tales, by way of the tremendous "Taras Bulba" and the black humor of *Dead Souls*. Without forgetting the plays and letters of that incredible Tartuffe, the man himself.

In Gogol's world, Tartuffe would have created Molière. This is something Private So-and-So would never have understood if he'd let others carry out his chore.

The army likes to celebrate feats of arms.

All this soldier leaves behind him are two alexandrines, carved high up into the cast iron of a flush, which rank among the most sumptuous in all of French poetry:

Yes, I can honestly say—sit down, pedagogue—
That I've read all of Gogol, right here in this bog.

(For his part, old Georges Clemenceau, "the Tiger," another famous soldier, paid homage to a chronic bout of constipation, without which, he claimed, he wouldn't have had the pleasure of reading Saint-Simon's *Mémoires*.)

8. *The Right to Dip In*

I dip in, you dip in, let's all go ahead and dip in.

It is our right, as readers, to grab a book from anywhere on our shelves, open it wherever we like, and dive straight in, just for a few minutes, because that's all the time we've got. Some books lend themselves more readily to this sort of picking and choosing, especially those with short, self-contained passages: the complete writings of Alphonse Allais or Woody Allen, the short stories of Kafka or Saki, Georges Perros's *Papiers collés,* the great La Rochefoucauld, and most poets . . .

That said, open Proust, Shakespeare, or Raymond Chandler's *Selected Letters* anywhere, dip in, and you won't be disappointed.

When you don't have the time or the means to treat yourself to a week in Venice, why not spend five minutes there?

9. The Right to Read Out Loud

Me: "Did your parents read out loud to you when you were a little girl?"

Her: "Never. My father traveled a lot, and my mother was much too busy."

Me: "So how come you like reading out loud?"

Her: "School."

Delighted that someone's got something positive to say about school, I burst out: "Aha! You see!"

Her: "It's not what you're thinking. School *banned* us from reading out loud. They made us read silently, even then. Direct from the eye to the brain was the theory. Simultaneous transmission. Quick, efficient. With a comprehension test every ten lines. Analysis and commentary from the word go. Most of the kids were scared witless, and that was just the beginning. I got all

the answers right, as it happens, but back home I'd read everything aloud."

"Why?"

"Because it was so amazing. The words sprang to life as I said them and took on an existence outside of me. It felt like an act of love. It was love. I've always thought that a love of reading is directly linked to love itself. I'd tuck my dolls up in my bed, where I was meant to be, and read to them. Sometimes I fell asleep at their feet, on the carpet."

I'm listening to her, and it's as if I'm hearing Dylan Thomas, drunk on despair, reading his poems in those cathedral tones. . . .

I'm listening to her and I can see old Dickens, bony and pale, close to death, stepping up onto the stage, his illiterate audience suddenly frozen, a hush so silent you can hear him opening the book . . . *Oliver Twist*, the death of Nancy. He's going to read us the death of Nancy!

As I listen to her, I can hear Kafka laughing through his tears as he reads *Metamorphosis* to Max Brod, who isn't sure he's following it properly . . . and I can see the young Mary Shelley reading great chunks of *Frankenstein* to Percy and their dumbstruck friends. . . .

I'm listening to her, and Martin du Gard appears, reading *Les Thibault* to Gide. But Gide doesn't seem to be listening. They're on the banks of a river. Martin du Gard reads, but Gide's looking somewhere else, his gaze is wandering—over there, where two teenage boys are diving, their perfection lit up by the water. . . . Martin du Gard is livid. But, actually, he has read well. Gide's heard everything, and he tells du Gard what he likes about those pages—though perhaps he might change this and that, here and there. . . .

And then there's Dostoyevsky, who didn't just read out loud but *wrote* out loud too. Dostoyevsky, breathless after shouting his indictment of Raskolnikov (or Dmitri Karamazov, I can't remember which now). Dostoyevsky asking Anna Grigorievna, his stenographer and wife, "Well? What's the verdict? Eh?"

Anna: "Guilty!"

And the same Dostoyevsky, after dictating the plea for the defense: "Well? Well?"

Anna: "Not guilty!"

Yes . . .

It's strange that reading out loud is a dying art. What would Dostoyevsky have said about it? Or Flaubert? Do we no longer have the right to put the words in our mouths before cramming them into our heads? No more straining our ears to hear? No more music? No more saliva? Don't words taste of anything anymore? Where on earth are we heading? Didn't Flaubert bellow his *Bovary* till he nearly burst his eardrums? And wasn't he then definitively in the best position to appreciate how sense comes through the sound of words, releasing meaning? Didn't he know better than anyone else, having wrestled with the arrhythmia of syllables and the tyranny of cadences, that meaning needs to be articulated out loud? What's the alternative? Silent texts for disembodied spirits? Give me Rabelais! Give me Flaubert, Dostoyevsky, Kafka! Give me Dickens! Come forth, great trumpeters of meaning! Come forth and breathe life into our books! Our words need making flesh! Our books need life!

Of course, there's something safe about silent words. You don't risk dying like Dickens, carried off after one of his exhausting public readings. Just us and the text . . . all those words silenced in the cozy solipsism of our minds. We sit knitting silent commentaries, feeling we're really somebody. And if you judge a book as something entirely separate from yourself, you don't risk being judged *by* it. Because as soon as your voice is involved, the book has plenty to say about its reader. The book says it all.

When someone reads out loud, they lay themselves wide open. If they don't know what they're reading—if they don't understand the words—it's excruciating, and you can hear it. If they refuse to inhabit what they're reading, the words are just dead letters, and you can smell it. If they saturate the text with their own personality, the author pulls back, it becomes a circus trick, and you can see it. The person who reads out loud is utterly exposed to the eyes of those who are listening.

If they're *really* reading, if they draw on all their knowledge while making sure they don't get carried away, if they are as sympathetic to the audience as they are to the work and its author, if they can make us hear the imperative to write while waking our deepest need to understand, then the book will open wide, and the crowd who thought they were excluded will rush in after the reader.

10. *The Right to Be Quiet*

We human beings build houses because we're alive, but we write books because we're mortal. We live in groups because we're sociable, but we read because we know we're alone. Reading offers a kind of companionship that takes no one's place, but that no one can replace either. It offers no definitive explanation of our destiny but links us inextricably to life. Its tiny secret links remind us of how paradoxically happy we are to be alive, while illuminating how tragically absurd life is. So our reasons for reading are as strange as our reasons for living. And no one has the right to call that intimacy to account.

The rare adults who gave me the gift of reading have always stepped back and refrained from asking what I understood. And of course I talked to those people about what I'd read. To all of them, living or dead, I dedicate these pages.

*The translator would like to thank
Caz Royds and Genevieve Herr at
Walker Books for their inspiring
and unstinting collaboration.*

—

The publisher gratefully acknowledges the use of the following material:

Chapter 25: Excerpts from *Madame Bovary*, by Gustave Flaubert, translated by Margaret Mauldon, published by Oxford University Press, 2005. The second extract has been modified by the insertion of a line from the 1981 translation by Gerard Hopkins, published by Oxford University Press. Chapter 31: Excerpt from *The Turning Point*, by Klaus Mann, published by Berg Publishers, Oxford, 1984. Reprinted by permission of the publisher. All rights reserved. Chapters 43, 44, and 45: Excerpts from *Perfume*, Patrick Süskind, translated by John E. Woods, published by Penguin, 1987. Chapter 47: Excerpt from *One Hundred Years of Solitude*, by Gabriel García Márquez, translated by Gregory Rabassa, published by HarperCollins, 2003. Chapter 47: Excerpt from *Adolphe*, by Benjamin Constant, translated by Carl Wildman, published by Curwen Press, 1948. Chapter 56: Excerpts from *The Habit of Being*, by Flannery O'Connor, published by Farrar, Straus & Giroux, 1979.

Every effort has been made to secure permission for the use of copyrighted material. If notified of any error or omission, the publisher will gladly make the necessary correction in future printings.